Manifest Your Highest Destiny

There are a lot of astrology books that talk about your character, talents, and challenges, but don't do much to answer the really big questions: *Why am I here, and how can I fulfill my life's mission to the fullest?*

Astrology for Self-Empowerment is filled with specific guidelines to help you answer those questions, and then to act on those answers. It presents the real power of astrology as a tool for achieving an intense inner transformation into the person you were born to be.

Dovid Strusiner presents the principles of Sacred Astrology, affirming that your place in the Universe is achieved by fulfilling your deepest desires and greatest potentials. He reformulates the ancient symbols for modern relevance, resulting in a system of astrology that is as practically useful as it is spiritually uplifting.

D15594 71

About the Author

Dovid Strusiner was born in London of Russian, Polish, and Jewish heritage. His family emigrated to New Zealand in the early 1960s. While still in his teens Dovid became immersed in both the Eastern and Western spiritual traditions. He has been involved in the study and practice of astrology for over twenty years. Dovid currently resides in New Zealand where he teaches, practices, and writes on Sacred Astrology.

To Write to the Author

If you wish to contact the author or would like more information about this book, please write to the author in care of Llewellyn Worldwide and we will forward your request. Both the author and publisher appreciate hearing from you and learning of your enjoyment of this book and how it has helped you. Llewellyn Worldwide cannot guarantee that every letter written to the author can be answered, but all will be forwarded. Please write to:

Dovid Strusiner
℅ Llewellyn Worldwide
P.O. Box 64383, Dept. K644-0
St. Paul, MN 55164-0383, U.S.A.
Please enclose a self-addressed stamped envelope for reply,
or $1.00 to cover costs. If outside U.S.A., enclose
international postal reply coupon.

Many of Llewellyn's authors have websites with additional information and resources. For more information, please visit our website at www.llewellyn.com

ASTROLOGY FOR SELF EMPOWERMENT

TECHNIQUES FOR RECLAIMING YOUR SACRED POWER

DOVID STRUSINER

2000
Llewellyn Publications
St. Paul, Minnesota 55164-0383, U.S.A.

FIRST EDITION
First Printing, 2000

Cover design by William Merlin Cannon
Editing and book design by Eila Savela

All horoscope charts used in this book were generated using WinStar © Matrix Software

Library of Congress Cataloging-in-Publication Data
Strusiner, Dovid.
    Astrology for self-empowerment : techniques for reclaiming your sacred power / Dovid Strusiner.— 1st. ed.
        p. cm.
    Includes index.
    ISBN 1-56718-644-0
    1. Astrology. 2. Self-actualization (Psychology)—Miscellanea. I. Title.

BF1729.S38 S77 2000
133.5—dc21   00-057486

Llewellyn Worldwide does not participate in, endorse, or have any authority or responsibility concerning private business transactions between our authors and the public.
    All mail addressed to the author is forwarded but the publisher cannot, unless specifically instructed by the author, give out an address or phone number.

Llewellyn Publications
A Division of Llewellyn Worldwide, Ltd.
P.O. Box 64383, Dept. K 644-0
St. Paul, MN 55164-0383, U.S.A.
www.llewellyn.com

 Printed in the United States of America on recycled paper

This book is lovingly dedicated to the memory of four star-light beings, most especially to my beloved son, David Jeffrey, who demonstrated the ultimate in courage, trust, and unconditional love. To my father, Jeffrey, who generously provided the precious gifts of freedom of choice and encouragement for my chosen pathway. To my dear friend, Gael Snow, who showed just how generous and loving one can be. To Tymon Duval, who brought me the gift of clear vision and just as quickly departed.

This book is also dedicated to two star-light alchemists. To my partner, Leeann, without whose insistence this book would never have manifested. For your encouragement, faith, and way of being, I give thanks. To my daughter, Shekinah, who never once minded her father being an astrologer and never complained throughout the creative process of this book.

The Sun and the Moon

O Thou Poet, great and primal in the rhythm
of Thy thought,
The Sun and the Moon arise and move
toward their setting;
The stars, shining like bits of gems,
are the fair characters
In which Thy song is written across the blue
expanse of sky.

Contents

Illustrations

Tables

Acknowledgments

I would like to offer my thanks to some very special people for their encouragement and loving assistance over many years. My mother, Pamela—thank you for your implicit trust, unconditional love and support for my pathway. Antony, your assistance over the years has been monumental. Your help with this work was inspiring and instrumental. Ricki and Joy, your loving support and generosity over the years has been wonderful. Gregory and Lawrence, you have always been the truest and dearest of friends.

Some other special people also need to be mentioned: Tracey and Vicki Feast, wild mountain sisters; Jo Roffe, the most delightful little white witch; Victoria and Rick, so generous with time and assistance; and Christopher, for timely crystals and loving encouragement.

Thanks also to Sha Fuller, Ian Rogers, Stephan Delaney, John Warren, Murray Langham, Robert Frost, Steve and Krystyna Upstill, Jane Melser, and David Brand.

I owe a special debt to Ann Kerns, Nancy Mostad, Eila Savela, and Bill Cannon at Llewellyn Publications.

I wish to thank all my clients who have taught me so much and who have helped me to see more clearly the wisdom and truth of the ancient art.

Finally, I wish to thank those great astrologers of the twentieth century who paved the way for the transformative and empowerment approach that I have been guided to promote.

Introduction

Alchemy is nothing but the art which makes the impure into the pure through fire.

—Paracelsus

The most dynamic and exciting spiritual transitional phase in world history is upon us. We are living through a period of unprecedented individual and planetary evolutionary development. It's a time when vibrant new spiritual threads are being woven into the fabric of human consciousness and interaction.

Consciousness is the defining element in our lives. In order to facilitate the unfolding of a new consciousness—the rebirth and reenactment of our true identity—we need to access the most vital, creative, and spiritually dynamic archetypes inherent in the collective unconsciousness of humanity.

Astrology, as the most ancient and profound of archetypal structures, stands on the brink of a renaissance. To meet the challenges of the new millennium, astrology is transmuting itself into a sacred art of self-discovery. Its beautiful language, for centuries seemingly inert and lifeless, is being transfigured into an alchemy of living symbols.

Its symbols now speak of psycho-spiritual transformation, regeneration, and wholeness; they can be used to redefine our consciousness and identity as human beings.

The central theme of this book is self-discovery, transformation, and empowerment through the application of astrological archetypes. To distinguish this holistic approach from the more traditional astrological practice, the phrase, the "astrology of self-empowerment," has been coined to clearly and succinctly describe an astrological pathway which emphasizes the psycho-therapeutic dimensions and the inner transformational potentials of the birth chart.

When we align ourselves to the archetypal patterns of our innermost nature through the practice of the astrology of self-empowerment we live a truly authentic life. We become willing participants in a sacred dance full of meaning, beauty, and spiritual intrigue. As we dance in harmony with the celestial sphere we bear witness to the birth of a new astrology. Out of the star-light a new psycho-therapeutic art of healing and self-discovery emerges; Sacred Astrology is born.

Sacred Soul Alchemy

The astrological archetypes exist as part of the collective unconscious of humanity. They embody an awesome potency of psychological transformative power. These ancient and primordial symbols, the *signs* of the zodiac and the *planets*, veil the initiatory passage that we all travel through on our personal and collective spiritual evolutionary journey. Wise women and men have long recognized the potentially significant role that a humanistic or person-centered astrology can play in the process of personal unfolding and self-empowerment.

Beyond the delusional future predictions, inane personality readings, and crass newspaper horoscopes that so often masquerade as astrology, there lies a significant and coherent symbolic structure. This symbolic structure is the real astrology, which is founded upon the zodiacal and planetary archetypes: primal and mythic symbols. They form the basis of the astrological art, whether practiced therapeutically or researched on a theoretical level.

The astrology of self-empowerment emphasizes that you are a unique being, with amazing possibilities that are beautifully symbolized in your birth chart, and that you have direct and unlimited access to the powerhouse of an abundant and intelligent universe which always provides guidance and the resources that are necessary for the fulfillment of your highest destiny. According to this approach, you are a drop in the ocean of an infinite Divine Being—a fragment of the totality of existence—an existence which recognizes no inherent difference between your perceived inner and outer worlds. To quote from chapter 5:

> *You were born in a moment of time, at a particular place, because the all-encompassing harmony and wisdom of the universe dictated that you fulfill a specific need of that moment. The need of the moment carries within itself both the fulfillment of the need, and its essential spiritual meaning. This is the greatest gift of astrology to you—an archetypal life-pattern which contains within its center essential human meaning made specifically for you.*

Sacred Astrology can help you to understand your life's purpose and actualize your innate life potential. By using age-old techniques of psycho-spiritual transformation, including affirmation, invocation, crystal energy transformation, and visualization, the text will show you how to transmute erroneous patterns of subconscious behavior and conditioning that are clearly symbolized in your birth chart. These are the patterns that may hold you back from expressing all that you are capable of being. By participating consciously in this transformational process you become a cocreator, a willing and joyous participant in your own spiritual odyssey.

By the application of *will* and *self-conscious awareness*, combined with the appropriate techniques of astrological self-empowerment, you are able to take the first steps towards manifesting your highest destiny. This is the alchemy spoken of in the ancient texts. It involves the magical transmutation of the gross personality, which perceives itself to be a separate being in time and space, into the pure Self which knows itself to be an eternal and infinite Consciousness. Sacred Astrology is a true alchemy that uses the universal symbolism of the celestial sky as the chalice in which our precious psychic ingredients are transmuted into pure soul gold.

The Renaissance of Astrology

Astrology awaits its renaissance in the heart of each of us. In a world that's crying out for greater spiritual meaning and a sense of wholeness, astrology has a very special role to play. For in its highest and purest form the profound symbolism of the celestial language can be used to help us find greater meaning. Meaning grows out of an understanding of our place and part in the universal order. Meaning is born out of a deep and heartfelt recognition of our undifferentiated oneness and interconnectedness.

Thus, an understanding of astrological concepts can aid in the development of impersonal love and compassion. Astrology also encourages patience and poise by providing ongoing insights into the rhythmic and cyclical nature of our lives. Finally, it can help establish harmony and peace in our lives. This is born of the equanimity that infuses our lives when we align with our Higher Self.

Actualize Your Full Potential

The astrology of self-empowerment isn't predominantly concerned with "who you are," at the idiosyncratic personality and event-orientated levels, but more essentially with "who you can be" emotionally, mentally, and spiritually, if you were to dedicate yourself to the pathway of self-discovery and empowerment, and let the inner transformative process flow freely in your life. Through this process you can manifest the seed potential symbolized in your birth chart.

While the approach taken in this book is a consistent development of astrology as it's usually practiced, the idea that there are specific exercises, techniques, and therapies that we can use to help actualize our birth potential is a radical and innovative extension of the usual astrological practice.

Self-discovery and empowerment through astrology tacitly implies a spiritual approach to life. Living the spiritual life may involve reaching beyond the purely personal into higher states of consciousness and peak experiences, but it may also imply a descent of spiritual force and power that focuses itself in and through us. This power, symbolically at least, descends from the celestial sphere.

Significantly, in the astrology of self-empowerment, the goal is not necessarily personal happiness (in any event, we cannot become happy, we can only *be* happy), nor the fulfillment of egotistical desires. The goal is effectively focused action that results in greater purity, personal integration, and wisdom. This newfound wisdom, in turn, leads us towards a deeper understanding of what it means to be a whole human being and, ultimately, we manifest the beauty of our divine archetype. At this most auspicious point in the process of self-actualization we have reclaimed our Sacred Power and become a pure channel for the Light of Life.

Astrology is destined to play an important role in our evolving planetary life—not because it has been around since the dawn of time, not because it has been studied and practiced by some of the greatest minds of every century, and not even because it's an astounding and profound symbolic language—but because, at its heart, it has an unmatched capacity to aid us in the process of psycho-spiritual regeneration.

A Spiritual Pathway

The astrology of self-empowerment is a spiritual approach to living. It is founded upon the concepts of oneness, divine harmony, impersonal love, and compassion. However, it's neither esoteric nor occult. There is nothing hidden, exclusive, or secretive about it. It's an uncomplicated and intrinsically inclusive person-centered pathway that seeks to encourage a mode of living through which we learn to demonstrate a natural and spontaneous flow of creativity, vitality, compassion, and loving interaction.

Because of its inherent simplicity there is no need to create convoluted spiritual paradigms and no discussion of higher or more subtle planes of existence, secret initiations, or knowledge gained by adepts.

Neither is the astrology of self-empowerment overly scientific and technical. Because of this, there will be some individuals—astrologers among them—who will dismiss this approach as being nebulous and unscientific.

The Power of Our Consciousness

According to the spiritual teachings of the centuries, and more recently in physics, not only are we all interconnected in a dynamic, pulsating web of divine life and thought energy, but astoundingly, our individual thought processes seem to be identical with the primary substance out of which the whole universe is created. This incredible truth was discovered centuries ago by the ancient Richis of India. These wise, Self-realized men and women called this mind energy *chitta*. They declared, unequivocally, that whatever thoughts we hold powerfully in our consciousness, if they are nurtured daily with strongly felt emotion, manifest sooner or later in our lives. Simply put: *potencies produce precipitation*. Powerful currents of thought create dynamic manifestations in matter.

If we desire to change our lives through the practice of Sacred Astrology (or any other technique), we need to change the nature of the thoughts and emotions that we allow to impinge upon our consciousness moment by moment. In order to change our circumstances we need to radically repolarize our consciousness.

It's amazing how rapidly some of our thoughts manifest. Thoughts are really the foundation of our reality. When our consciousness is supplanted with new, vitalized thoughts and pure emotions it becomes like a mental dynamo. It electrifies and vivifies our capacity for creative living and abundant manifestation.

The nature of our thoughts and feelings underpins our lives. By virtue of their purity, clarity, and power we weave the fabric of our seemingly separate existence. It will become clear, upon an examination of your birth chart, that there is a synchronistic relationship between your thoughts and feelings, and your birth chart potential. If nothing more, our birth chart is a clear and concise map of the type of thoughts and emotions that we perennially hold in our consciousness. The problem for most of us (as stated in an ancient axiom) is that *mind is the slayer of the real.* That is, by the use of our conscious and subconscious minds, we confabulate all kinds of apparent realities. In order to achieve a degree of wholeness and self-empowerment, we need to discriminate between habit patterns that we have created—the complexes, neurosis, and psychosis of our psychology—and our pristine and eternal true Self.

Walking On

Walking the astrological pathway towards greater self-empowerment implies developing a freedom, wholeness, and psychological purity that is the antitheses of the habitual patterns described above. The "walking on" will often involve a dramatic reorientation of our usual way of life. The implication is that, sooner or later, a revolutionary adjustment in our consciousness and, consequently, in our way of life takes place, through which we seek to become a more pure channel for the Light of Life. Through directly participating in this transmutational process we are able to fully actualize our highest birth chart potentiality. In so doing we reclaim our Sacred Power and manifest our highest destiny.

By living with little or no understanding of our thoughts and the power they have over our lives, many of us abdicate, at least temporarily, our sacred strength as a divine archetype in time and space. Unfortunately, we were never taught about the fundamental relationship between our thoughts, our emotions, and our life manifestations—nor how to affect changes in our lives. However, through the ancient symbolism of the celestial sky, the universal forces are always waiting to rally around to help us on our life's journey.

As you begin to use the zodiacal and planetary archetypes to transmute and purify old patterns of being, events and circumstances will tend to get behind you. Remember, you are always supported and nurtured by the loving kindness of the universal intelligence. It's a magical and sublime intelligence which can, and does, make all things possible.

Our Uniquely Individualized Mandala

Each of us has a unique birth chart pattern, our very own individualized birth mandala. As well as symbolizing our highest destiny and potential, it also symbolizes the problems, tests, issues, and unfinished business that we are likely to encounter in our life journey. At the deepest level, we all face similar archetypal battles, and the keys that unlock your hidden potential and allow the process of self-empowerment to take place are the same keys that have been used for millennia. In one form or another, astrological self-empowerment is a well-trodden pathway.

The archetypal battles of life may be similar for all of us, but the existential manifestations—our specific life events, circumstances, and dramas—remain absolutely unique to us. Until they are upon us they usually remain unpredictable and—at our present level of evolutionary development—unknowable.

Our inner transformative process may involve a lifetime of struggle and search or we may find that under the clear focus of our consciousness we achieve our hearts' desires rapidly. With the appropriate techniques, sustained effort, and the grace of God it's possible to speed up our natural evolutionary process.

By the practical application of the techniques of the astrology of self-empowerment you can take steps towards reclaiming your Sacred Power and manifesting your highest destiny. In doing so, you will naturally radiate the dynamic positive polarity of the symbolism shown in your birth chart. The astrological techniques outlined in this book will show you how to achieve this goal.

Prologue

*I*n the beginning, out of the Radiant Darkness, on which
naught can be said, there streamed forth, like a flash of
lightning, the One and the All, a Dreamer of Dreams, a
Weaver of Spells, a resplendent eternal Consciousness, our Lord
and Master and our true Mother and Father—a vast Being
embodying the sublime state of absolute Existence.

This Light of all the Worlds exists and has always existed
throughout all the dream cycles of countless manifestations—
breathing in and breathing out, ever alternating in our world
of duality with Her day-force and Her night-force.

In absolute Awareness the all-knowing and ever-present One
sounds the Word and breathes Life into Her Mind's creations.
By Her power of all-bewitching Maya She sustains everything
that is, in all states and conditions.

Within the perfect simplicity of the One there developed a myriad of complex relationships throughout the worlds, yet always underlying this complexity there remained an inherent interconnectedness, harmony, and balance.

Knowing from the beginning Her precious creations' need for meaning and awareness of loving harmony, She bestowed upon the child dreamers of the dream a most magical gift. In the celestial sky She created an eternal, archetypal, symbolic language. This most ancient and beautiful gift to the child dreamers of the dream is now called the zodiac.

1

The Magic of Astrology

*Understand that you are a second world in miniature, and the
Sun and Moon are within you, as are the stars.*
—Origen, *Homiliae Leviticium*

The celestial sky peers down upon us nightly. It silently and
unceasingly radiates its cosmic message of harmony, beauty,
and meaning. It subtly conveys amazing truths—eternal truths that
can be found hidden within the age-old body of astrological lore.
One of the most incredible truths is that there is a real link, an
observable parallelism, between the timing of events in the celestial
sky and our unfolding lives.

Astrology is an ancient and enduring archetypal structure—
ancient and enduring enough to have witnessed and withstood the
rise and fall of great civilizations. Archetypal because it is rooted in
the depths of our collective unconscious. Astrology is a profound and
sublime celestial art. When practiced in its highest sense, with
integrity, sensitivity, and wisdom, astrology can help us gain a greater
sense of order, significance, and Self in a seemingly chaotic and
frightening environment.

Throughout the ages, the wisest of the wise have believed in, studied, practiced, and taught astrology. Great women and men have spent their lives in pursuit of astrological wisdom and understanding. Plato, Aristotle, Plotinus, Ptolemy, Copernicus, Galileo, Brahe, Kepler, and Newton practiced astrology. Civilizations as diverse as the Egyptians, the Indians, the Babylonians, the Greeks, the Chinese, the Japanese, the Incas, the Chaldeans, and the Tibetans, among others, have embraced astrology in one form or another.

Astrology: Capturing a Moment of Time

Yet, because astrology deals with concepts, forces, and symbols that refuse to be pigeonholed by the limitations of our analytical mind, it eludes modern science's attempts to prove or disprove its validity. Try as we may, we don't yet understand the modus operandi of the inner workings of astrology. Fortunately, we don't have to completely understand how astrology works in order to make positive use of it. Is it not enough that we can use astrology to gain insight, some small perception of order, and a deeper understanding of our place and part in the pageant of life?

As well as not fully understanding how astrology works, many of us have enormous difficulty trying to grasp even a modest comprehension of just what astrology is. The task is anything but easy, for astrology has been and continues to be, in some respects, a cocktail of religion, spirituality, psychology, psychotherapy, philosophy, and metaphysics.

Paradoxically, astrology concerns itself with moments of time and with timeless realities, with beginnings and endings and the pathway between, with the part and with the whole, with the relative and the absolute. These dichotomies may be responsible for some of the misunderstanding and confusion that inevitably arises in any discussion of astrology, and it tends to increase the reluctance of many scientists to seriously examine the art. However, research is being done that builds upon that which has already taken place in the twentieth century. It is only a matter of time before the scientific community will begin to study astrological concepts in depth.

Astrology is an attempt to orient us in the universe and, as such, it's unlikely it will ever become a pure science. The scientific mind looks everywhere, including outer space, for facts and the ultimate knowledge of life, but typically has failed to see that the answers are under our very nose. To search for the meaning of life in subatomic particles or in outer space is to avoid the search where it's perhaps most critical—in our consciousness. The real issue and task for the sciences of the new millennium will be to seek the integration of our inner and outer worlds in our consciousness.

One of the stumbling blocks to a greater openness and inquiring attitude towards astrology is that the ramifications of accepting astrological concepts are monumental. They throw many of our prized ideas about the universe and our place in it upside-down. For this reason, emotions usually run high when any discussion of astrology ensues in contemporary academic or religious circles.

Yet, despite these difficulties in understanding and a general lack of mainstream scientific acceptance, astrology continues to call many to its pathway. A pathway which, in its purest form, is concerned with aiding and quickening our inner transformative processes through the use of universal symbolism.

Whether astrology actually functions in a symbolic, causal, synchronistic, or other as yet unknown way, is beside the point from the perspective outlined here. The real solution to our problems, at whatever level they may occur, whether physical, emotional, mental, or spiritual, whether collective or individual, is dependent not upon science and technology nor upon the reasoning power of the mind. Solutions are dependent upon our ability to express in ever-increasing ways the unifying energies of harmlessness, harmony, and impersonal love. This is precisely where astrology's strength lies.

A Shift in Consciousness

In its beautiful and unusual symbolic language—the code of the stars—astrology speaks to us of the energies of synthesis and integration, and of their place in our lives.

If we are to ever change the likely script of our human destiny (contrary to popular belief, the deeper teachings of astrology neither encourage nor subscribe to a fatalistic or deterministic approach to life), it is imperative that we individually and collectively transform our inner lives. To achieve this we need practical techniques for personal and group empowerment capable of making major shifts in consciousness.

In its highest form, astrology contains a spiritual, transformative power. It becomes a measure of our capacity to become more than man, more than woman.

The Archetypes

Astrology provides us with dynamic self-discovery and empowerment tools in the form of the zodiacal and planetary archetypes. The astrological archetypes are our common human legacy. They are primordial images which carry and embody our conceptions of the world in which we live. Archetypes reoccur time and again throughout human history in the form of myths and psychic impressions. Although far more difficult to identify than our common symbols, archetypes are primal expressions of the underlying energy patterns that guide and shape our lives.

These prototypical patterns, symbols, and images of psychic force have lain dormant—in our minds—either in complete slumber or in a semicomatose and incoherent state. It is time for astrology to walk out of the shadow and to stand clear and strong, radiating its message of universal order, harmony, and meaning amidst the difficulties that confront us individually and collectively.

Astrology was born of humankind's need for harmony and order in a seemingly hostile and confusing environment. The fundamental techniques for reclaiming our power that astrology provides are as ancient as the symbolism itself. Let's go on a psychological and spiritual voyage of self-discovery and reclaim our Sacred Power. Many of us embody personal paradigms that have become so rigid and distorted that mental and emotional crystallization has taken place.

Sacred Astrology can help us to refine, transmute, and regenerate our debilitating mental and emotional patterns.

We Create Our Own Destiny

Before we commence our journey and learn about the astrological archetypes and the specific techniques of astrological self-discovery and empowerment, let's look at an erroneous notion that we all embody occasionally. The notion is that something or someone else is responsible for our life problems, for our failed dreams, or for our inadequacies. We may blame our parents, teachers, partner, children, or a deprived childhood environment. It could even be the limitations supposedly ordained by our "stars."

Facing Self in the Timeless Moment

The natural human tendency is to point the finger rather than to take personal responsibility and face Self. This is precisely what astrological self-empowerment is all about. It is about facing Self and transforming patterns of emotional and mental energy that hold us back from expressing all that we are capable of being.

The Self is that essence within us which is never born and never dies (as opposed to the egotistical self of our personality). It's the eternal "I Am That I Am," described in *Vedanta* as Existence-Knowledge-Bliss-Absolute. In the context of the astrology of self-empowerment, facing Self requires being aware of, and then removing, obstacles that inhibit us from experiencing our pure and inherently all-knowing and all-loving true essence. The idea of facing Self and embracing transformation (of self) sounds relatively straightforward, yet few of us seem to be ready to demonstrate the requisite honesty and resolve to "walk on."

A Symbolic Universe

Carl Jung, one of the twentieth century's greatest psychologists, stated in the foreword to the book, *The Secret of the Golden Flower:*

"Whatever is born or done this moment, has the qualities of this moment of time." The qualities (or energies) of the moment can be deciphered from the symbols of the celestial sky, i.e., through the language of astrology.

Humanity is steeped in symbols. Symbols evoke a response from us at an unconscious, instinctive level. They bring together mental and emotional associations that defy our logical or rational mind. Without symbols we couldn't even communicate with each other, for language is but an incredibly complex mass of symbols. Yet, in our modern and so-called sophisticated times, many people ignore, or deride as of no importance, the most ancient, vast, and magnificent symbols that exist. These are the symbols of the celestial sky. It appears that in the modern rush to dissect and analyze the mysteries of the universe under our mental microscope, we are in danger of losing a holistic and synthesizing perspective which would provide the very answers we seek.

Sacred Astrology

The zodiac, which is one of our greatest archetypal symbolic structures, developed over many centuries. Originally, the zodiac grew out of early man's fascination with the constellations; it is now usually determined by the apparent path of the Sun around Earth (the *ecliptic*).

The zodiac contains living symbols that embody powers that we can unleash in our lives. These twelve individual symbols are called the *signs* of the zodiac. They are archetypal patterns of rhythmic and cyclical activity for our solar system.

Against the celestial backdrop of the signs of the zodiac, the *planets*, by their location and juxtaposition, represent multiple functional energies of psychological integration and emergence. Modern astrology analyzes and interprets the positions of ten planets, including the Sun and the Moon, which are called "planets" in astrology.

The planets symbolize specific dynamics of our psychological makeup. For example, the Sun in our birth chart correlates with our creative life-force and with our individuality. In order to create the positive changes in our lives which we desire, the zodiacal archetypal forces will be used in combination with planetary forces and proven age-old methods of transformation.

At the time of our birth, the planets, by their web of mathematically determined interrelationships, symbolize the complexity of our patterned psychology. These planetary interrelationships are called *aspects*. Astrology uses numerous aspects to detail the complexity of our psychology and potential.

The planets and their aspects at our birth form a complex algebra of our psychic life. In order for us to decipher this algebra of life we require not only formulae and the ability to interpret them but, more importantly, we need to develop our intuition. We need to sensitize ourselves to our unfolding life story and seek out the real meaning behind the circumstances. Only if these qualities of sensitivity and intuition are present can we successfully use Sacred Astrology as a pathway that leads to self-actualization.

To be self-actualized means to become a whole person. It implies a degree of freedom from the collective and from an unconscious bondage to the values of our family, nation, and culture. The moment such an implication is understood, a basic change occurs; a reorientation and development in our psychology takes place—it leads sooner or later to a new approach to life and to astrology.

The planetary positions and aspects coincident at our birth contain, in coded form, the seed idea or the blueprint of our inherent individuality. This blueprint, which combines zodiacal and planetary positions and their interrelationships (as well as the ascendant and the houses), is called our *birth chart*. It's determined by our time, date, and place of birth. Our birth chart, natal chart, or horoscope (from the Greek *horoskopos*, meaning "hour pointer") is simply a two-dimensional representation of the three-dimensional reality of celestial space at the time and place of our birth.

As above, So below

Poetically, we could say that at any given moment the planetary forces resound with a multidimensional, multifaceted gong tone that reverberates throughout our solar system, calling to life all those of us who resonate to that particular melody-of-being. When we are born a matrix of individuality is created. In its archetypal or seed form it resides with us for life.

The popular view paints astrology as a fatalistic and character-based art that's more concerned with sensational predictions and personality trivia than with personal development and unfolding. What needs to be realized is that there is a huge amount of profound astrological lore that has been developed over thousands of years. Today, many astrologers and others in the healing professions, including psychotherapists and psychologists, apply astrological principles with sound judgment and sensitivity. In spite of this, some people still believe that astrology is just another New Age practice through which, with a little bit of hocus-pocus planetary power and the right astrologer, miraculous life-enhancing pronouncements can be received.

Fortunately, most of us realize that real personal growth and self-empowerment don't come so easily. In the words of an old saying: "For a tree's branches to reach to heaven, its roots must reach to hell." There can be no coming to greater self-awareness and higher states of consciousness without struggle and difficult life experiences. There are no shortcuts and magic cures—astrological or otherwise. Nor can any astrologer take away the need for individual effort and personal responsibility. In its deepest sense, our birth chart is meant to be a reflection of our life pattern and potential, not a means of avoiding it.

Trust, Purity, and Openness

Although there are no easy routes that lead us towards self-empowerment, divine grace always flows, and if we believe in our Self and have pure motives, all things are possible. There is a beautiful story in Buddhist literature that describes how a low-caste barber one day heard the Buddha speak of Nirvana (a sublime and blissful cosmic state of consciousness) and afterwards rushed up to him and asked expectantly, "But could I, a barber, reach Nirvana?" The Buddha answered, "Yes, even you, a barber." Immediately, the man reached Nirvana.

Whether this story is true or not doesn't matter. The salient lesson is that we hold ourselves back from psycho-spiritual transformation by our limited patterns of thinking and by our attachment to erroneous emotional and mental conditioning.

As soon as we are able to demonstrate a clear resolve and openness to change and progress, all doors tend to open and grace can flow into our lives. Such resolve may come through meeting a person or through a major life event. It may be the culmination of many years of personal struggle or be the instantaneous recognition of a new need we feel. At this pivotal point in our unfolding, we often seek guidance and the appropriate technique or pathway to aid us in the process of change and self-empowerment. Astrology is one such technique and pathway and is arguably the oldest, and still one of the best.

2

Celestial Self-Discovery

Formation, transformation, Eternal Mind's recreation.
—Goethe, *Faust*

When it appears that all is lost the turning point is often very close to hand. The story has been told in many ways throughout the ages, from the myth of the rising of the phoenix, to the dark night of the soul. As so often happens in life, at the point of our greatest despair and anguish, there may come a moment of stillness at which the way is revealed and solace and comfort are found to ease our pain. Call it by what name we may, there is a voice that speaks where there is none to speak. It is the voice of the silence, the influx of divine grace. Out of this auspicious moment new hope is born. Strength and vision return.

One of astrology's greatest gifts is that major growth periods and crises in our life are often clearly symbolized in our birth chart by what are known as the *transits* of the planets, specifically those of the trans-Saturnian planets: Uranus, Neptune, and Pluto. Transits are the current positions of the planets in the celestial sky as they relate to the planets in our birth chart by the mathematically determined aspects or interplanetary relationships.

The inner meaning of the psycho-spiritual crisis and the potential for transformation is indicated in archetypal code by the transit(s) but the existential details, the particular events, are never revealed, though they may be surmised or, worse still, guessed at. Maybe it is as it should be that the process of inner change is often surrounded by a mystery which has a subtle beauty peculiar to itself.

We Create Our Future in the Eternal Now

Astrological prediction, even at an archetypal level, is not always easy. It may be possible to accurately predict the crowing of a rooster each morning at a particular time, but the prediction of a major crisis or life development, its inner meaning, its possible future ramifications, and its immediate solution are far more complex. Such prediction and analysis demand a mixture of perceptive intelligence, intuition, and understanding which is naturally rare in any human being.

This leads directly to one of the major flaws in astrology as it's so often practiced today. There has been a total misunderstanding between the concepts of archetypal potentiality, as indicated in symbolic form by our planetary configuration at birth, and the working out in our life of the archetype, as shown by our physical, emotional, mental, and spiritual manifestations.

The particular and the specific should never be deduced solely from our birth chart. If they are, it's likely to be delusional and inaccurate. This form of fortunetelling is a dangerous distortion of the sacred art. The tendency to use all kinds of predictive techniques to try to make judgments about our future life is singularly pernicious and likely to be highly destructive. These kinds of readings, by and large, only succeed in planting negative seeds of ideas in our subconscious mind. There is rarely anything positive that transpires from such an encounter, and the only likely beneficiary is the charlatan-astrologer.

The event-orientated predictive techniques just described have no place in the astrology of self-empowerment. On the contrary, they are delusional and potentially destructive techniques that rob us of our personal power. Astrological self-empowerment is founded on a wholly different approach. It emphasizes our capacity for free will, subject only to the archetypal restraints encoded in our birth chart.

We Become the Path

As we embark upon our voyage of celestial self-discovery not only will we develop and practice our unique therapeutic method of Sacred Astrology, we will become the method. What is of paramount significance is our level of awareness, purity of motive, and dedication to transformation. In a very real sense, when we desire strongly enough to empower ourselves, we become our very own transformative catalyst. As we live the alchemical life we become the path and the magical stone of the wise. We reclaim the Jewel of Eternity.

If we steadfastly embrace an astrological therapeutic process (as outlined in this book), we can potentially take our first tentative steps towards either changing our reality or repolarizing our mental and emotional states, so as to embody a greater acceptance of our situation. Total understanding is born of total acceptance.

All of our crises can be used for positive growth. All situations are unique and particular, but the crisis will always bring the solution. The need is always fulfilled on one level or another at the right time.

A Conscious Approach to Life

For astrological self-discovery and transformation to transpire within us, two components stand out as being absolutely necessary for a successful and meaningful outcome. First, we need to develop an understanding of the cyclic nature of our lives. In other words, timing is critical. Without an intuitive awareness and insight into our natural developmental process, we can not flow with major life changes. If we lack awareness of or attempt to avoid working with these critical transitional phases, we will tend to develop a psychic resistance which leads to greater inner tension, anxiety, and fear.

It is crucially important that we learn to understand something of the archetypal meaning of the major transits and progressions. Undoubtedly, transits and progressions are astrology's best techniques for determining what phase or cycle of life we are passing through. While a traditional astrologer may use transits and progressions as methods of event prediction (with very modest success), a modern-day astrological therapist is more likely to employ the techniques as a method for pinpointing our important life developments and for gaining insight into our inner cyclic process.

The second component absolutely necessary for astrological self-empowerment is our conscious awareness. This has two aspects: our capacity to adequately meet the life challenge with a clear awareness of the potential opportunity offered by the crisis, and a willingness to consciously participate in the crisis with the intention of using the experience to take the next step in our personal unfolding. It's important that we recognize the real demands of the crisis situation, and that we exhibit determination to move through the experience in a positive, life-enhancing way.

Reclaiming our Sacred Power through astrology is totally dependent upon the two factors of timing and awareness, for the practice of astrology, in its purest form, demands a conscious approach to life. The astrology of self-empowerment's desired outcome of personal integration and self-empowerment requires of us a dedication, purity, and resolve to face a crisis with courage and expectation. This naturally makes strenuous psycho-spiritual demands upon us.

Seek out the Way with Wisdom

Only when the traveler reaches the destination may he or she prudently put aside the map (birth chart). Even then, it's wise not to burn it for there may be another time when, once again, the battle must be fought, when the sea of confusion, ignorance, and fear needs to be navigated again.

It's said in the ancient teachings that great ones on the brink of divinity occasionally fall back, unable to withstand the challenges of the moment. If this is the case, we ought to walk on with modesty and humility, realizing that, until the final victory has been won, we should use whatever means are at our disposal to seek out the way with wisdom. In this way we align ourselves with the ever-unfolding harmony of the universal order.

Great use can be made of the transits of Uranus, Neptune, and Pluto in astrological therapeutic work. These trans-Saturnian planets, in their highest symbolical context, can be viewed as messengers from another galaxy, who mysteriously and inexorably call forth the inhabitants of our solar system to the path of total transformation.

Uranus, with its scintillating moments of illumination, infuses our minds with thoughts and realizations that, while coming through us, are not of us. Neptune, by slowly but surely dissolving worn-out patterns of our consciousness, leads us to lose sight of our self in the all-encompassing, universal Self. Pluto, by its unfathomable and methodical pulverization of the old emotional and mental life, thrusts us kicking and screaming into a new mode of living.

So, the process of individual unfolding goes on in one form or another. If there is anything predestined in life it's surely that we are all to participate in an amazing drama, whose script we help write and rewrite, and where we play our scenes either dutifully or unwillingly. We act out our roles, struggle with the script, misbehave like spoiled starlets when confronted by crises, and finally, if we are wise, we consciously align ourselves to the loving kindness and the vision of the director.

3

Astrology for
Self-Empowerment

*The soul of each single one of us is sent, that the universe may
be complete.*

—Plotinus, *Enneads*

Even with a cursory look at the huge amount of literature on
astrology, what strikes the perceptive mind is that hardly anything at all has been written on specific techniques and exercises
which will assist us in actualizing our birth chart potential.

The situation is ironic because to most astrologers the whole art
and practice of astrology is about helping individuals to unlock
their innate potential. If this is so, why should the literature provide
so little in the way of specific transformational exercises and
empowerment techniques? There are numerous excellent books on
astrological transformation. They detail all of the technical aspects
of the process, its timing and severity, the nature of the encounter
and its likely effect on our lives, and many more factors, but the
obvious is usually omitted.

We need to not only understand mentally why we are going
through a process of change, whatever it may be. More importantly,
the process needs to be integrated and fully embraced into the totality
of our being. It must become a part of our very atoms.

Embracing a Deeper Understanding

Only through fully embracing a crisis is real meaning established, as opposed to an intellectual understanding of a difficult or traumatic life experience. Ultimately, we need to develop a deeper understanding of our specific life crisis—its inner meaning and ramifications—and, eventually, let an acceptance of the process permeate our consciousness. Total acceptance allows an inner peace and poise to illumine our consciousness. Under these conditions real psycho-spiritual growth takes place.

It is evident that for a small proportion of astrological practitioners and their clients the practice of astrology has little to do with inner transformation and personal development and more to do with superficial, inane personality readings and frivolous, potentially damaging predictive work. However, it's important to differentiate between this kind of practice and the true art. When the great Indian spiritual master Paramahansa Yogananda was once asked if he told people's fortunes, he replied that he found it far more useful to mend people's fortunes. However, for some individuals, the bizarre landscape of the astrological world provides fertile ground for a kind of mental paralysis in which the fatalistic concepts of destiny and fixed character become an excuse for mental and spiritual laziness.

A significant and often overlooked facet of our free will is that life always avails us of the opportunity to enter into and to consciously participate in our major life developments. Transformational life experiences are not thrust upon us by the vagaries of "the stars," nor are they experiences that just happen by accident. We need not be an impotent participant, a bystander, or a victim as we walk through life.

We Are the Controlling Center

We are, potentially, both the controlling center and the dynamic point of self-awareness that determines how a crisis or an event is integrated into our consciousness.

Support for this idea comes from an unexpected quarter. The new physics—quantum mechanics and relativity—suggest that rather than merely impotently observing the dance of life, we are, in some sublime and mind-bending way, the center, the cocreative and controlling essence. In the new physics, we find a rerun of the ancient mystical teaching that states that each and everyone is a Being of Light, whose center is everywhere and whose circumference is nowhere.

By participating consciously in these great moments of cyclic unfolding we truly flow in and through life. As the great Chinese philosopher Lao-tzu said: "Live life as life lives itself." If it's accepted that we contain within ourselves the symbol and the meaning, the vision and the goal, then all that remains is for us to walk on with ever increasing purity, determination, and wisdom, and to allow the magical moments to transform us.

Our Subconscious Mind and the Planets

In order for the alchemy of Sacred Astrology to transpire we need to consciously work with the forces of our subconscious mind.

Every day of our life, in a multitude of ways, we speak to our subconscious mind, and curiously it accepts everything we tell it. When we wake up in the morning and say to ourselves, "It's a lousy day, I want to go back to bed," it believes us. Furthermore, it tries hard to recreate a lousy day for us whenever our conscious mind is amenable to the idea. We don't even have to speak plainly to it. Any subtle suggestion or hint will suffice. It happily does the rest for us.

The trouble for most of us is that what we tell our subconscious mind is in complete opposition to manifesting and living a fully empowered life. All too often we generate unhelpful or self-destructive patterns in our subconscious mind simply by our lack of awareness of the process. Clearly, we need to use all our shrewdness and mental dexterity to work positively with our subconscious mind in order to initiate positive psychological patterns and circumstances in our lives.

Our subconscious mind and the planetary forces symbolized in our birth chart have a longstanding and interesting relationship. There is a link—a synchronistic relationship—between our planetary symbolism at birth and our subconscious patterning. Hinted at here is one of the keys to a deeper understanding of our psyche and an aid to overcoming the pull of the past. There is only one fundamental difference between our subconscious patterning, our conscious life experiences, and our planetary positions at birth. The sole differentiation lies in our capacity to manifest free will and self-conscious awareness.

In order to transform our erroneous emotional and mental patterns and to fully empower ourselves, what is required is the will and self-conscious awareness, together with the appropriate practical techniques.

Techniques of Sacred Self-Discovery

The most potent techniques for making major shifts in our subconscious patterning have been around (like the archetypes) since the dawn of time. Among the most effective are affirmation, invocation, suggestion, symbol, crystals, and visualization.

If these techniques are used together in a unified way, the potential transformative energy becomes enormous. The second half of this book describes these techniques and their therapeutic use when combined with the zodiacal and planetary archetypal forces. These are the techniques for reclaiming your Sacred Power through astrology.

There are five steps that lead to astrological self-empowerment:

- Step one involves learning about the signs, planets, houses, and aspects, and their part in the practice of Sacred Astrology.

- In step two you will be introduced to the specific techniques of the astrology of self-empowerment, including affirmation, invocation, visualization, and crystal energy transformation. As you study these techniques you will learn how to affect fundamental changes in your psycho-spiritual nature.

- Step three teaches you how to find the major themes and potential in your birth chart. This knowledge not only allows you to determine which planetary and zodiacal symbols to work with to affect sacred soul alchemy, but significantly, it also facilitates learning to unleash your creative force and invoke the healing energy within.

• Step four is the design of your personalized astrological program of self-change—a program centered upon your major themes, patterns, and inner potentiality. At this point in the process you decide which areas of your life you wish to work on. You also choose specific exercises and therapies from those provided (affirmations, invocations, visualizations, and crystal energy therapies) or you create your own personalized exercises and therapies.

• Step five is the ongoing practice of the techniques of Sacred Astrology.

The planetary energies symbolized in our birth chart form a bridge which links our self-conscious state to our subconscious mind and from there to the collective unconscious where the zodiacal archetypes reside. The planetary and zodiacal archetypes find their synthesis in the superconscious state—our divine Self.

The signs of the zodiac and the planets are awaiting our use in the process of self-empowerment. By affirming, visualizing, and calling upon these archetypal forces, we are able to traverse the bridge between our inner worlds. In time we can purify, redefine, or resolve erroneous patterns within our consciousness. We can also initiate positive new life-enhancing patterns. If we are really daring we may even reestablish the link with the superconscious state, our Sacred Self.

4

The Signs of the Zodiac

The Earth is bound up in some necessary way with the local motions of the heavens, so that all power that resides in this world is governed by that above.

—Aristotle, *Meteorologica*

Throughout our lives the signs of the zodiac impact our unfolding consciousness. As we assimilate the lessons of each sign we are led towards a deeper understanding of our psycho-spiritual energies and what it means to be a whole human being.

The signs of the zodiac not only reside in the celestial sky. Significantly, they are to be found, in their essential psychic form, in the collective unconscious of humanity. This truth is subtly but beautifully expressed in the ancient dictum: "That which is above is as that which is below."

An Individualized Mandala

The zodiac represents the formative realm of our psycho-spiritual life. It's a rich tapestry interwoven with ancient meanings and mythic symbols. As we have seen, the major themes of our psychic life are revealed, in star-code, by our zodiacal and planetary configuration at birth. However, life isn't static. We all participate in a dynamic and ever-changing journey of self-discovery through the entire circle of the zodiac.

Our birth chart is in a state of constant flux. It ebbs and flows with the great lunar, solar, and planetary cycles. It is an ever-changing symbol—a uniquely individualized mandala flowing with the cyclical movements of the planets. When we interpret our birth mandala with wisdom and persistently apply astrological self-empowerment techniques, we journey towards greater awareness and personal empowerment. Ultimately, we reenact our true nature.

We Are the Beginning and the End

Each sign of the zodiac embodies a cosmic principle or divine idea. The signs detail twelve characteristic phases of our unfolding. While traditional astrologers and the general public like to equate the signs of the zodiac with quite separate and specific characteristics it's helpful to see all twelve signs as parts of a whole (figure 1).

The signs of the zodiac are simply twelve phases relating to the cyclical and rhythmic unfolding of human life. These phases are totally interdependent and interrelated, both in the abstract and in the realm of human experience.

We embody all twelve signs of the zodiac in differing degrees and at different levels of integration. We mysteriously experience both the part and the whole. We are the beginning (Aries) and the end (Pisces) and the totality of the path between the two.

In any meaningful interpretation of our birth chart we should attempt to evoke a clear picture of the whole of our individuality. This means relating our zodiacal influences (planets in signs) to the phase of the whole zodiac cycle. To focus predominantly upon the complexity of the parts would at best be inadequate, and at worst a travesty of the astrological art. The whole always takes priority over the parts.

For example, you may have your Sun in Capricorn and understand something of the personality traits of this sign, but what does

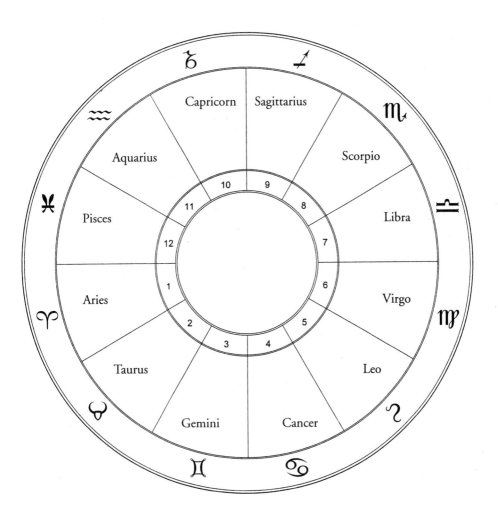

Figure 1. Signs of the Zodiac

a Capricorn Sun really mean in terms of your overall spiritual development and future pathway? In other words, it is more important to understand how Capricorn fits within the whole cycle of the zodiac than to have confirmation of a myriad of personality idiosyncrasies.

The Signs of the Zodiac

The following table of symbols, principles, and keywords shows how the signs of the zodiac describe the whole cycle of creation. The twelve signs of the zodiac, their symbols and their correspondences tell us, in the coded language of the celestial sky, the meaning of the cycles of human existence. They describe the rhythmical and holistic nature of our life on this beautiful planet.

Table 1. Signs of the Zodiac

Sign	Symbol	Principle	Keywords
Aries	♈	Action	Initiative and Impulse
Taurus	♉	Reaction	Appreciation and Stability
Gemini	♊	Interaction	Awareness and Adaptability
Cancer	♋	Containment	Protection and Caution
Leo	♌	Individuation	Dominion and Power
Virgo	♍	Differentiation	Discrimination and Service
Libra	♎	Equilibrium	Harmony and Love
Scorpio	♏	Transformation	Depth and Regeneration
Sagittarius	♐	Vision	Wisdom and Understanding
Capricorn	♑	Crystallization	Order and Responsibility
Aquarius	♒	Distribution	Universality and Liberality
Pisces	♓	Redemption	Synthesis and Compassion

Triplicities and Quadruplicities

Traditionally, the signs of the zodiac are divided in several different subgroups. The two most important are called *triplicities* (or "elements") and *quadruplicities* (or "modes"). These subgroups derive from the division of the zodiac into groups of four and three respectively.

Triplicities are the age-old elements of fire, earth, air, and water. Fire signs are intrinsically active, fiery, and assertive. Earth signs exhibit a practical and stable influence. Air signs are communicative and intellectual. Water signs are emotional, instinctive, and intuitive.

Table 2. The Triplicities

Fire	Earth	Air	Water
Aries	Taurus	Gemini	Cancer
Leo	Virgo	Libra	Scorpio
Sagittarius	Capricorn	Aquarius	Pisces

Quadruplicities are derived from the division of the zodiac into cardinal, fixed, and mutable signs. Each grouping expresses a different quality. Cardinal signs are outgoing, fixed signs are naturally resistant to change, while mutable signs are adaptable and versatile.

Table 3. The Quadruplicities

Cardinal	Fixed	Mutable
Aries	Taurus	Gemini
Cancer	Leo	Virgo
Libra	Scorpio	Sagittarius
Capricorn	Aquarius	Pisces

Table 4. The Triplicities and the Quadruplicities

	Fire	Earth	Air	Water
Cardinal	Aries	Capricorn	Libra	Cancer
Fixed	Leo	Taurus	Aquarius	Scorpio
Mutable	Sagittarius	Virgo	Gemini	Pisces

Aries: The Ram

Ruler: Mars
Element: Fire

Aries represents the birthplace of divine ideas. It is the archetype of will and emergence.

Aries symbolizes the beginning of a new cycle of manifestation and life experience. It's the seed shooting out of the ground in springtime. The sprouting of the seed through the crust of the earth is a beautiful symbol of Aries. It forces its way towards the light of the Sun while carrying within itself a pattern which details its type and quality.

The Arian archetype evokes within us the principle of birth and action. The inherent nature of life is to externalize itself, to make manifest its latent possibilities. As an Aries we see life as being full of promise and hope. Demonstrating supreme confidence, we assert ourselves positively through direct action and initiative.

The symbol for Aries represents the horns of the Ram. This is indicative of our urge towards impulsive, self-assertive action and it represents our desire to initiate new endeavors with incredible vitality and power. We embody the spirit of the pioneer. As a spiritual warrior we are determined to exercise complete personal autonomy in achieving our chosen ideal or in following our dream.

Ideas are particularly important for the Arian, who is forever emphasizing the development of the intellectual faculty of human consciousness. The concept of emergence is also pivotal. Yet, with the impulse to emerge come many fears and insecurities that only time and experience will allow the Arian to overcome. The emotional instability, instinctive and self-absorbed character of the adolescent (Aries) must eventually be transmuted into the ruby heart and diamond consciousness of the fully empowered and mature adult (Pisces).

In Aries we demonstrate the principle of cosmic individuality. We are the fire of mind behind which lies the synthesizing energy of Oneness and Unity. Our innate strength and confidence gives rise to great daring and courage. We seek action for its own sake and embody a will to freedom, a fear of constraint, and a dislike of systems and hierarchy.

Taurus: The Bull

Ruler: Venus
Element: Earth

Taurus is the archetype of divine desire because it functions at the level of emotion and security.

If Aries is the symbolic fountainhead of manifested life, Taurus is the steadily flowing river that provides the multitudes with sustenance in the fertile soils. Taurus is the archetype of cosmic stability and certitude.

In Taurus we learn to harness the vitality of Aries. As we take initiation out of the Arian fire our boundless exuberance meets the solid resistance of Taurean power. Instinctively, we feel impelled to put Arian energy to practical use.

Our pioneering and driving Arian mental energy is now directed toward seeking emotional peace, poise, and love in Taurus. In Aries we surged forward with reckless abandonment; in Taurus we hold back and stabilize our gains. The Ram meets the Bull.

The symbol of Taurus conveys its inherent fertility and receptivity. As the Arian seed impregnates the fertile Taurean Earth Mother, a divine creative process is born. Out of the womb of the earth emerges emotional depth and security seeking. Aries has expended its resources too readily and enthusiastically. Now it's time for the Taurean to conserve and seek a more bountiful supply.

In Taurus our emerging self-consciousness learns to move ahead in complete certainty and stability. We demonstrate remarkable reliability and steadfastness. Shaken to the very core, we still stand strong, for we embody the primal essence and raw strength of Taurean power.

In Taurus our mission is to consolidate Aries' emerging seed and send down deep roots to anchor ourselves into the earth. We seek a sustainable and durable life experience. Our instinctive nature drives us to seek tangible results and, in the process, we learn that results are gained through constant repetition, insistence, and undeviating effort.

The Taurean desire for emotional and physical security—the fruits of the earth—takes over from the pure, but insecure, Arian urge towards conquest and action. Our pioneering instinct gives way to the settler's organizational urge. The determination, self-will, and fixity of purpose of the Taurean may lead to a closed mind, which emphasizes self and forgets our social and collective responsibility. In its lower manifestations, this primal earth energy expresses itself through a static and stubborn resistance to change and progress.

As a Taurean we learn how to generate real and demonstrable power—to make things happen on the physical plane, to build, and to sustain. Our adolescent Arian urges for excitement and stimulus give way to the force of tradition, habit, and inertia as we adapt to the Taurean phase of the cycle of existence.

Gemini: The Twins

Ruler: Mercury
Element: Air

Gemini is the archetype of divine awareness and distinctiveness. It represents the fusion of opposites and the intelligent work of unity and synthesis.

In Gemini we approach the last stage of the spring of human unfolding. The Taurean phase of the cycle of the zodiac has taught us how to feel deeply and maintain a stable existence. Yet, now we feel a yearning for new directions and interests. Our unfolding soul rebels against the stuffy constraints of the preceding phase and we seek stimulus and excitement in undiscovered realms of the mind.

In Gemini the action and reaction of Aries and Taurus give way to interaction. Our Geminian capacity for intellectual awareness and insight enables us to see meaningful patterns and designs in our life.

The archetype is of a developing analytical mind that seeks to relate to both ideas and people. The communication of ideas becomes one of the most prominent themes for Gemini. There is a continuous process of learning and intellectual development. Facts, systems, numbers, and specifics become increasingly important.

As we absorb the lessons of Gemini we realize that everything has a distinct and useful purpose, even the smallest and most obscure particular. As such, the capacity for detailed analysis and love of knowledge—as opposed to wisdom—and the interrelationships between things and ideas captures our imagination. The parts are in danger of becoming more important than the whole as our intellect races forward and concocts new worlds based on knowledge gained.

In Gemini we seek a rapid development of mind and an interplay with other minds. This may be expressed through learning, teaching, and the communication of ideas. We experience a potent desire for personal and intellectual stimulus beyond the seemingly stagnant realm of the Taurean phase.

The ability to classify, to logically understand, and to manipulate a multiplicity of thoughts and concepts, begins to develop within the Gemini phase of our life experience. In the deepest sense we experience a process in which thought becomes a means of growth.

In Gemini we are a mental magician who uses words, names, and logical ideas to convey newfound truths of our life experience. However, all of this thought is in danger of leaving our evolving consciousness feeling slightly insecure and vulnerable. Because we have not yet developed a clear sense of our own individuality, we develop many different kinds of relationships to avoid a confrontation with Self.

If in Taurus we seek emotionally secure relationships, in Gemini we build a diverse range of stimulating, mental relationships.

In Aries we are the individualistic spiritual warrior, in Taurus we call forth the primal earth man or woman, and now in Gemini we learn to develop a sense of the interrelatedness and interplay of the worlds. We become the exemplar of the adaptable magician.

Cancer: The Crab

Ruler: The Moon
Element: Water

Cancer symbolizes the principle of cosmic protection. It is the archetype of the divine feminine.

In Cancer the Sun reaches the climactic point of its yearly cycle. This is the summer solstice (in the northern hemisphere). The Sun has progressed as far as it can go and now, crab-like, it retreats.

The Cancerian archetype denotes containment, receptivity, and fluctuation. Cancer is the Great Mother who nurtures and protects her children. The symbol for Cancer brings to mind the breasts—a primal symbol of both fertility and sustenance. Indeed, traditionally this sign is said to rule the breasts and stomach. Cancer is a symbol of the "womb of space," and impregnation in Cancer comes nine months before the birth of the soul in Aries.

In the symbol of the Crab we have a creature of the sea, a creature born of the unconscious forces of life. Its movements are somewhat regressive and it appears to sidestep rather than seek confrontation. Its hard shell protects a soft and delicate interior. All these qualities are mirrored in the characteristics of Cancerian individuality.

As we attune to Cancerian energies we mirror within our consciousness the psychic and unconscious forces of life. Because these gigantic forces can easily overwhelm our still fragile psychology, we erect protective barriers in order to keep our still embryonic individuality safe. Visions, dreams, religious feelings, intense love energies, and strange experiences assail our sensitive Cancerian psyche. We seek solace and security in the familiar and the traditional. Family and community life provide us with the necessary safe haven for our evolving soul, for the instinctive, the biological, and the irrational can only be safely tolerated in small amounts.

In Cancer we become weary of the constant stimulus and mental gymnastics of the Gemini. Our deepest need is bodily nourishment and real soul contact. The extension in all directions of Gemini gives way to a deliberate focus on formative life-energies and the need to set boundaries. The constant desire for new and stimulating relationships is reversed. We retreat to the comfortable, the secure, and the well-trodden byways of life. This may lead to crystallization of our ego with the resultant fear, insecurity, anxiety, and oversensitivity or it may lead us, potentially, to an inner freedom, joy, peace, and exaltation. This is the highest destiny of the Cancerian.

Leo: The Lion

♌

Ruler: The Sun
Element: Fire

Leo represents the principle of cosmic splendor. It is the archetype of divine strength and dominion.

The symbol for Leo is open, flowing, and very dynamic. It suggests that as Leo we are self-expressive and extroverted as opposed to our Cancerian past where we exhibited self-repressive and introverted tendencies. Throughout the preceding life experience in Cancer we were concerned with two basic issues. The first was a clear and deliberate focusing of our life-energies towards self-protection and psychic nourishment. The second was an acceptance of the responsibilities inherent in our family, culture, and nation.

Leo sees a progression of this second idea. In Leo we seek to demonstrate a higher level of social awareness and responsibility. Social issues and relationships take precedence as we try to merge within the collective for the first time. As we scintillate with Leonine power the natural shyness and instinctive caution of Cancer gives way to a pronounced social conscience and a desire for group participation.

Leo develops our creative impulses. This, in turn, gives rise to a new dimension of our personality. We embark upon our life's adventure to manifest a great vision or a dynamic personality. We may express the rampant individualism of the artist or the inspirational charisma of the leader. We strut, posture, or parade on whatever stage we can find, but deep within we simply hunger for greater acceptance, meaning, and self-assurance.

In Cancer we learned how to express and acknowledge our feelings and biological needs. We also learned to accept our personal limitations and inadequacies. Now, as Leo, the energies are reversed. We feel internally impelled to seek the limelight. The mantle has somehow befallen us and we boldly step out onto the world stage to demonstrate our newfound social conscience and capacity for spirited leadership.

We express a dramatic extroversion of our personality, but deep within we may still harbor feelings of personal inadequacy. Why else would we seek such inflated recognition and immodest display?

In its higher arc, Leo's nature manifests a fair degree of magnanimity and generosity, while in our less-developed brothers and sisters we see the pretentious, grandiose, pompous, and egotistical behavior that has become the hallmark of Leo. Through all the games and role-playing we seek, above all, a greater sense of personal identity. Leo is the archetype of seeking security at the level of personality and social interaction. The process of self-actualization is now in full force.

Virgo: The Virgin
♍

Ruler: Mercury
Element: Earth

Virgo symbolizes the principle of cosmic perfection. It is the archetype of purity, discrimination, and integrity.

Each sign of the zodiac contrasts with its predecessor and none more so than Virgo and Leo. The Virgoan phase of the cycle of the zodiac leads us out of Leo, with its self-expressive and demonstrative disposition, into a phase of quiet introspection and discreet discipline.

The mystery of Virgo's discipline is conveyed in the enigma of the sphinx. This mythological creature, half-Lion and half-Virgin, veils the mystery of initiation out of Leo into Virgo. An initiation out of the egotistical phase of individuality into a new phase of purification, analysis, discrimination, and service.

In order to wield power safely we must, once again, become of pure intent. Our inherent and essentially pristine nature is regained in the sign of the Virgin. Yet, the sphinx also contains the power of the Lion. This suggests that one of the fundamental lessons of Virgo is the embodiment of both purity and strength. The raw power and strength of the Lion is transmuted into pure reason and discrimination in Virgo. While this combination of strength and purity is a rare commodity in our world, it's nonetheless the highest ideal of the Virgoan archetype. This combination is attained through learning humility and wisdom under the guidance of a true teacher.

In Virgo we become the apprentice. We eventually attain mastery and regain our lost purity by applying the right techniques steadfastly in a methodical and detailed way. By the application of right technique, as learned from a true teacher, we are able to repolarize our immature emotional and mental expressions (as exemplified in Leo), and regenerate our nature.

Some of Virgo's excesses are an inordinate devotion to petty and minute detail, a lack of perspective to encompass the whole, a fanatical adherence to particular systems of diet and health, and a way of life that lacks joy and spontaneity. However, in Virgo we always have the opportunity to acquire new skills. True to Virgo's meekness and humility, we usually attain mastery in quiet obscurity. At this climactic point in the process of self-actualization we step forward and are initiated into the realm of the collective as symbolized by Libra.

Libra: The Scales

♎

Ruler: Venus
Element: Air

Libra represents the principle of cosmic harmony. It is the arche-type of social interaction, equilibrium, and relationship.

While the first six signs of the zodiac deal primarily with individual unfolding, the second six are concerned with the evolution of the collective consciousness of humanity. They emphasize the structure of human relationships and our place within the greater whole.

As the autumnal equinox approaches, the days and nights are of equal length. Nature literally reaches a point of balance. The symbol of Libra, the Scales, beautifully represents this balance. Libra is the archetype of social values and justice as well as the sign that rules aesthetic and artistic appreciation.

Libra takes us out of the two previous phases of self-assertion (Leo) and self-criticism (Virgo). It leads us into a phase of self-consecration to humanity. In Libra we are challenged to become a willing and harmonious participant in the greater whole of humankind. As we travel this pathway we learn to develop the virtues of fairness, cooperation, and helpfulness towards others.

In Libra we operate as a cell within the organism of humanity. Our goal is no longer the development and assertion of personality, nor the achievement of any strictly ego-oriented goals. A major shift in consciousness has taken place—a shift that results in social and collective issues becoming more significant to us than purely personal issues.

Libra rules over marriage and all close, structured relationships, as well as the relationship between the individual and the collective. Human interconnectedness and interaction becomes our driving force and motive. We pour our precious psychic force into social values, processes, and ideals. Our minds and hearts are galvanized by the vision of Oneness and harmony as we seek to discover our true place in the overall play of life.

As Librans we stress social norms, values, and activities in the same way that Aries, often in an arrogant and exaggerated way, stresses the rights of individuals to express their inherent uniqueness and individuality. While we may be accused of having an exaggerated social conscience, this just emphasizes that we are prepared to make personal sacrifices for the benefit of the whole.

When we are caught up in the currents of Libran air we are willing to go to great lengths to fit into the established social hierarchy and be accepted as a worthwhile community member. This quality makes us something of a chameleon who can merge into different situations with ease. If our feelings of social responsibility are not adhered to, all kinds of fears, insecurities, and feelings of guilt may manifest.

At our core we are driven by a desire to seek a point of equilibrium. This desire leads us towards seeking group harmony and collective well-being. Because Libra is essentially a sign of evaluation the natural tendency is to weigh situations and people by referring them to acceptable social norms. In this way, social usefulness and the capacity to operate in an harmonious way become the standards we use to make evaluations.

Scorpio: The Scorpion and the Eagle
♏

Ruler: Pluto
Element: Water

Scorpio symbolizes the principle of cosmic purpose. It is the archetype of regeneration and transmutation.

The dual symbolism of the Scorpion and the Eagle suggests that Scorpio is capable of very different levels of expression and manifestation. In mythology, the Eagle becomes the phoenix, which rises from its own ashes. The Eagle's ability to soar higher than any other living creature makes it one of our greatest symbols of regeneration and resurrection.

In Libra we are galvanized by the vision of harmonious group activity. In Scorpio, that vision takes root in the depths of our emotional life and seeks full and total expression. Our emotional feeling nature is revitalized. We desire to feel and experience life at the deepest level of our psycho-spiritual nature.

As we walk Scorpio's thorny pathway our soul cries out for psychic purification and regeneration. Unlike our experience in Virgo with its emphasis on propriety, or our sojourn in Libra that became preoccupied with social niceties, in Scorpio we are ready to invoke a rebirth—a renaissance of our spirit. Disgusted and weary of our old, diseased patterns and experiences we ruthlessly attempt to eliminate the nonessential, the mundane, and the old. When life is stripped to its bare bones we are left with the most profound elements of human existence: sex, birth, survival, deep mental and emotional impulses, death, and the spiritual. In Scorpio, we come home.

Scorpio rules over the sexual reproductive force—the libido. In order for social harmony (as emphasized in Libra) to manifest, society needs to re-create itself. The driving force of evolution is now revealed and experienced at the core of our individuality. However, unlike Taurus where we experienced sex as a predominantly biological and procreative act, in Scorpio the sexual act becomes a way in which we can merge, at all levels, with another human being. In Scorpio our intense need to be individualistic is overtaken by an even more powerful primal desire to empathize and merge with another. The sexual act becomes our gateway to self-forgetfulness, and it potentially provides us with an experience of sublime states of awareness. In any event, we now hunger for more than mere sex.

Along the psycho-spiritual transformative pathway symbolized by Scorpio lie many dangers. They include the misuse of power, emotional and mental domination, cruelty, ruthlessness, manipulation, possessiveness, jealously, guilt, and fear. The path leading to psychic regeneration can be long and arduous.

In its higher manifestations Scorpio embodies the courage of Aries and Leo, the sharp mental processes of Gemini and Virgo, the perseverance and strength of Taurus, and the caring sensitivity of Cancer and Libra. It's little wonder this sign of the zodiac arouses awe, admiration, and fear in others. When the Scorpion magically transmutes itself into the Eagle all things become possible.

Sagittarius: The Archer

Ruler: Jupiter
Element: Fire

Sagittarius represents the principle of cosmic abundance. It is the archetype of vision and progress.

In ancient symbolism Sagittarius is represented by the Centaur: a half-man and half-horse creature who shoots his shafts skyward. The horse is a potent symbol of virile power that we can harness and ride. In Sagittarius we are impelled, metaphorically, to explore distant lands and to seek new adventures.

The process of collective development, which began in Libra with its code of right behavior and progressed in Scorpio with its emotional security-seeking, now leads us toward new mental and spiritual horizons. As we are reborn out of the depths of Scorpio's transfiguration a new vision takes hold. The arrow of the Archer signifies our new mental and spiritual vision.

Both Gemini and Sagittarius are intellectual signs. However, in Gemini we are primarily concerned with understanding the detailed interconnectedness and interplay of things, while in Sagittarius we are more likely to be absorbed in distant and subtle connections: the religious, the metaphysical, and the spiritual.

Sagittarius is the Centaur, not the Eagle, whose knowledge is gained from higher perspectives and secret places. As such, Sagittarians' belief structures, though anchored deep within their psyche, stem from the known and from structures inherent in society.

As we live the Sagittarian adventure, the collective still dominates and society's needs take precedence over the needs of the individual. In this phase of our development abstract ideas and ideals inspire us. Social movements, causes, and quests of all kinds captivate us. By virtue of our zodiacal inheritance we embody power and understanding. All that remains is for us to walk on.

The pure Sagittarian temperament is scrupulously honest, open, and direct, unlike Scorpio, which can be secretive and underhanded. The faults of the sign include exaggeration, self-righteousness, wastefulness, overoptimism, inconstancy, tactlessness, and fanaticism.

If we are daring enough to travel the highest Sagittarian pathway, life will provide us many opportunities to develop our creative vision. In this way we may inspire others. Then, as we prepare to take initiation into Capricorn's earth we merge with the great Centaur and reclaim our divine visionary power. At this most auspicious moment our consciousness soars to sublime levels. Coming down once again we recognize that it's our mission to shoot forth the fiery shafts of beneficence upon the whole of humanity.

Capricorn: The Goat

♑

Ruler: Saturn
Element: Earth

Capricorn symbolizes the principle of cosmic order. It is the archetype of the manifested spiritual force.

The eternal promise of spring lies dormant in the earthy temperament of Capricorn. As we take on the intense challenge of manipulating gross matter, our soul seeks, once again, to be reborn out of the crystallization of a previous cycle of existence.

Capricorn symbolizes the authority of the state over us. We experience the power of politics, organizations, and nations. We are challenged to assume a profession and maintain an ordered place within society.

Capricorn also symbolizes the perfected human being who has complete dominion over his or her bio-psychic energies—an individual who participates naturally and effortlessly in the greater life of the whole. Capricorn, in its highest spiritual context, symbolizes that auspicious moment when we are initiated into a direct awareness of the collective whole and with our true Self.

In Capricorn it's our task to concretize, to make manifest the abstract ideas of Sagittarius. By expressing the Sagittarian vision in a tangible form we are able to fulfill our destiny and complete our experience of the earth element. There is a time for everything and Capricorn (Father Time) is a master of timing. The qualities of patience, loyalty, self-sacrifice, responsibility, and perseverance are Capricorn's finest virtues.

In Aries we experienced an unconscious desire for childlike self-projection. In Leo we expressed the force of our personality in grand, egocentric ways. In Sagittarius the purely individualistic was superseded by a vision of wholeness. Now, in Capricorn, we carry within ourselves the potential to bring down the vision and to bring it into concrete manifestation. In Capricorn our highest goal is to live the life and demonstrate selfhood.

Capricorn, with its faults of inertia, selfishness, materialism, and lack of joy, carries within its womb the promise of the divine force. Lying deep within Capricorn's temperament the seeds of impersonal love and service to the world slowly germinate and in Aquarius they break through the hard crust of Capricorn's earth. Capricorn's structures can never be permanently set. Aquarian reformers wait in the wings to dismantle and build anew. Crystallization always gives way to reformation.

Aquarius: The Water Bearer

Ruler: Uranus
Element: Air

Aquarius represents the principle of cosmic distribution. It is the archetype of impersonal love and humanitarianism.

The seed of divine impersonal love that lay dormant in all but the most fertile of Capricorn earth begins to stir in rich Aquarian soil. If Capricorn, in its highest symbolical context, is the perfected human being who is initiated into a new order of existence, Aquarius symbolizes the spirit woman or man who comes down from the mountaintop and gives freely to humanity. The Water Bearer carries an urn out from which living waters flow that bring to life the highest ideals of humanity.

Power is always released in the fixed signs of the zodiac. In Aquarius we invoke the power of the creative spirit of humanity to substantiate the ideal, and power to manifest the perfect society. We effortlessly express our unique individuality within a social and collective context. We may be cranks peddling our peculiar brand of social policy, fanatics, eccentrics, rebels, or humanitarian reformers. Interestingly enough, the sign Aquarius produces more than its fair share of visionaries and intellectual geniuses.

In whatever way the drama plays out, Aquarian energies lead us from being merely a pawn of the state or a social automaton (Capricorn) towards pouring out our life-force in the cause of world service and uplifting humanity.

The vessel of the Water Bearer perfectly symbolizes Aquarius' capacity for selfless service and sharing. For the Aquarian, knowledge of the truth isn't a sufficient goal. The impulse is to disseminate knowledge to all. The Aquarian temperament is liberal, freedom seeking in thought and speech, humanitarian, impersonal, and endlessly curious about things and people. In Aquarius we operate within society as an equal among equals. Unlike our Leo brothers and sisters, we don't demand to be the leader, for we are intrinsically at ease in the social context.

Democracy and freedom of thought are the highest Aquarian truths. The concept of the brotherhood of man epitomizes our forward-thinking. However, in order for a new consciousness to fully empower all members of society the old structures must be totally ripped away. In achieving this end Aquarian forces can be highly destructive, even violent, but we pull down only to build anew.

The period of transition and rapid social reform that our planet is presently passing through comes under the Aquarian phase of the zodiac's cycle. Capricorn's rigid structures have begun to crumble. Conservatism and hard-line rule have been overtaken as the Aquarian vibration takes root in the mass consciousness of humanity.

Beyond these changes, Aquarians sense the presence of new life, but manifesting new life causes many hidden fears and insecurities to arise from within the individual. Some of the faults of Aquarius are an impersonal and uncaring attitude, rebelliousness for its own sake, selfishness, an overemphasis of the intellect, and a loss of simplicity.

Pisces: The Fish

♓

Ruler: Neptune
Element: Water

Pisces symbolizes the principle of cosmic grace and compassion. It is the archetype of redemption and universal love.

The last phase of the Sun's journey through the zodiac is reached in Pisces, the mutable water symbol of the Fish. In order to manifest the glorious visions of the highest Aquarian ideal, total dissolution of old patterns and forms is necessary.

In Pisces the comfortable and the familiar are ripped out from under us. There is no stability, no structure to cling to, no familiar safety net, and absolutely no security. We enter unknown and mysterious realms that ultimately lead us out of a completed cycle of human existence into evolutionary processes and cycles that can only be imagined.

Pisces is the sea of the Great Mother of life, ruled by Neptune. The sea is not only deep and beautiful, it can also be treacherous and violent. Pisces, like all the water signs of the zodiac, can erupt with the force of a tidal wave when aroused. The Piscean saint or adept also carries the sword of severance and dissolution.

The fleet-footed dancing feet of the Piscean almost never touch the ground. Emotional and psychic to the very core, this elusive archetype speaks of a new order of life. If Aquarian brilliance and spontaneity are analogous to nuclear fission, Pisces is fusion. Everything merges into unqualified Oneness. A clear and separate sense of identity is difficult to grasp because the Piscean is caught up in the collective consciousness.

The sign of the Fish is that of a world savior, an avatar of the highest order. The perfection of Capricorn's manifested divinity and Aquarius' divine spirit now attains the most sublime manifestation in Pisces. Perfect wisdom merges with perfect love. An anointed savior is born.

In Pisces we are asked to relinquish our reliance upon society—to stand alone and follow the inner voice rather than the dictates of the collective, to have unshakable faith in the face of the unknown and the unknowable, to settle all accounts, to leave the comfortable civilized Aquarian lifestyle behind, and to enter the wilderness of the natural forces and elements.

Everything is transcended in the sign of the Fish. All of the tried and true formulas of living are to be let go. In order to pass the final test of the zodiac we must stand strong and face Self. The delusions, complexes, and mental miasma that so often accompany the Piscean adventure are concomitant with letting go of the known and the trusted.

Our consciousness may be overwhelmed with all kinds of irrational fears, phobias, insecurities, and strange, unfathomable neuroses. We may seek escapism to offset our personal pain and the perceived tragedy of human existence. Yet, to pass our final initiation and progress, everything must be faced and accepted for Pisces is the archetype of total acceptance and total understanding born of compassion and divine love.

5

The Planets

Nothing exists nor happens in the visible sky that is not sensed in
some hidden moment by the faculties of earth and nature.
—Johannes Kepler, *De Stella Nova*

In the previous chapter, we noted how the signs of the zodiac symbolize the cyclical nature of our lives and, in particular, how each sign leads us toward a deeper understanding of our psycho-spiritual energies.

In contrast, the planets symbolize more specific dimensions of our mental, emotional, and spiritual energy field. Planetary energies represent dimensions of being and self-expression upon which we naturally focus. As we assimilate the lessons of the planets, we are better able to integrate and harmonize the various components of our complex psychology.

You were born in a moment of time, at a particular place, because the all-encompassing harmony and wisdom of the universe dictated that you fulfill a specific need of that moment. The need of the moment carries within itself both the fulfillment of the need, and its essential spiritual meaning. This is the greatest gift of astrology to you—an archetypal life-pattern which contains within its center essential human meaning made specifically for you.

The zodiacal archetypes form a stage—a celestial backdrop—upon which the planetary actors perform, according to our conscious and subconscious direction. Most modern astrological techniques, including the astrology of self-empowerment, use planetary positions as the basis for interpretive and therapeutic work.

Ancient and Mythic Symbols

The planets not only traverse the celestial sky, more significantly, they travel in their essential psychic form within the inner space of our subconscious mind. The planetary archetypes are mythic symbols, incredibly ancient, powerful, and primal. They affect our consciousness, most often with subliminal subtlety, occasionally with subterranean intensity.

The planets, by their position and aspects, symbolize the differing degrees of personal integration that we each embody. The following table of symbols, principles, and keywords indicates how the planets symbolize our inner psychic nature and the complexity of our emotional and mental life. The ten planets (by their symbolism and correspondences) tell us, in the coded language of the celestial sky, the meaning of our particular birth pattern. They describe the way in which we are able to express our uniqueness as human beings—how we may best express our Sacred Self.

Table 5. The Planets

Planet	Symbol	Principle	Keywords
Sun	☉	Power	Life-force and Spirit
Moon	☽	Response	Sensitivity and Fluctuation
Mercury	☿	Communication	Intelligence
Venus	♀	Harmony	Beauty and Relationship
Mars	♂	Action	Force and Projection
Jupiter	♃	Expansion	Optimism
Saturn	♄	Crystallization	Limitation
Uranus	♅	Change	Innovation and Radicalism
Neptune	♆	Transcendence	Compassion and Idealism
Pluto	♇	Transformation	Regeneration

Planetary Dignities

Traditionally, each planet has dominion over one or two signs of the zodiac. This relationship between planets and signs is called rulership. For example, the Sun rules Leo, while Venus rules both Libra and Taurus.

A planet is said to be in detriment when placed in the sign opposite to that which it rules and is deemed to operate in a weakened state when so placed.

Each planet also operates at its strongest in one sign. This is called the sign of its exaltation. The opposite sign is called its fall. The following table lists the traditional rulers, detriments, exaltations, and falls of the planets.

Table 6. Planetary Dignities

Planet	Ruler	Detriment	Exaltation	Fall
Sun	Leo	Aquarius	Aries	Libra
Moon	Cancer	Capricorn	Taurus	Scorpio
Mercury	Gemini Virgo	Sagittarius Pisces	Virgo	Pisces
Venus	Taurus Libra	Scorpio Aries	Pisces	Virgo
Mars	Aries	Libra	Capricorn	Cancer
Jupiter	Sagittarius	Gemini	Cancer	Capricorn
Saturn	Capricorn	Cancer	Libra	Aries
Uranus	Aquarius	Leo	Scorpio	Taurus
Neptune	Pisces	Virgo	Cancer	Capricorn
Pluto	Scorpio	Taurus	Pisces	Virgo

The Sun

Our Creative Life-Force
Ruler of Leo

The Sun is the archetype of power, vitality, and individuality.

Great Sun of life, light of our souls,
Source and support of all.
Come to us great shining One,
As we dance upon your sacred rays of splendor.
Show us your shining face.

The Sun represents the active and masculine dynamic that operates within each of us. Its principle is similar to the *animus* of Jungian psychology. As an expression and manifestation of the energies of Spirit on the physical plane, it symbolizes our self-awareness, power, and creativity.

The position of the Sun in our birth chart symbolizes our will and life-force and, as such, it mirrors the primal creative principle of life. The Sun (by sign, house, and aspects) enables us, potentially at least, to fully empower ourselves and rediscover our sacred essence. It's our link to the Source of All and so carries a promise of our Oneness and interconnectedness with all life.

Sun sign astrology may be a crude caricature of the true art but it does correctly emphasize that the Sun is the source and support of all our life energies—both biologically and spiritually. Our creative and vital essence is clearly symbolized by the Sun in our birth chart. In order for us to feel whole and fulfilled we need to let our solar power radiate freely.

The Moon

$\mathcal{D}$

Our Self-Image and Emotional Response
Ruler of Cancer

*The Moon is the archetype of fluctuation, passivity, and the
unconscious.*

> *Sister, Mother, Goddess,*
> *Wild and free,*
> *In playful darkened wombs of space,*
> *Dreaming tides of fancy.*

The Moon radiates no light of its own yet beautifully reflects in silvery glints the light of the Sun. It's the receptive and passive *anima*. The rhythmic ebb and flow of the lunar cycle mirrors the feminine reproductive cycle and hence, like Venus, the Moon is an archetypal feminine symbol.

The Moon in our birth chart symbolizes our self-image, as opposed to the inner spark of individuality and creativity of the Sun. Our self-image is not so much a conscious and clear perception of who we are, but an intuitive or unconscious response to our innate individuality. Thus, the Moon represents an image we have assimilated of ourselves by virtue of past experiences and psychic impressions.

Our personality is built upon the foundations of the past, and the Moon correlates to all past conditioning, especially our early family environment and relationship to our mother. It also symbolizes the fears, anxieties, and insecurities that we experience when we are still in the grip of unconscious forces. Lunar traits are characterized by the manifestation of instinctive, irrational, intuitive, self-protective, and nurturing forms of behavior.

Mercury

The Communicator
Ruler of Gemini and Virgo

Mercury is the archetype of thought, movement, and communication.

Truthful Hermes,
Wisdom your heir,
Flying high in Divine thought,
Living on wings of light.

Mythologically, Mercury is the messenger of the gods who, with winged feet and helmet, carries the caduceus of entwined snakes. Mercury is symbolic of mind and, as such, governs our intelligence, communication skills, rapidity of thought, and discrimination. All nervous system processes, as well as writing and language, also come under the rulership of Mercury. Thus, the position and strength of Mercury in our birth chart symbolizes our capacity for communication, learning, and teaching.

Mercury provides channels for the creative life-force of the Sun to radiate intelligently. He shows how we register and analyze the phenomenal world that constantly impinges upon our consciousness. Mercury also symbolizes mediation and the facilitator who brings people together to seek a reconciliation of opposites.

While the Sun represents our individuality and self-conscious awareness, Mercury allows for an interplay of dynamic thought. Through this process we learn new things and make interesting connections. Mercury's dexterous intelligence can both analyze and synthesize. It allows us to demonstrate both unified and analytical thinking.

Venus

The Power of Love and Beauty
Ruler of Taurus and Libra

Venus is the archetype of harmony, equilibrium, and peace.

Mother of mothers, most desirable one,
With loves strangest mystery dancing in your eyes.
Goddess of the dawn, Goddess of the dusk, come.

Venus is the passive and feminine planetary harmonizer. She integrates the parts and brings them together into a unified whole. Venus governs love, physical beauty, feminine sexuality, artistic processes, attraction, and affection.

As the mythological Roman goddess of love and beauty, Venus epitomizes our desire for creating acceptable social rules and aesthetically pleasing forms. Like the Sun, Venus is a creative principle. She gently leads us towards expressing our inner creative potential through diverse art forms. Venus correlates to musicians, artists, entertainers, diplomats, and romantics.

As the ruler of relationships in our birth chart, Venus symbolizes how we seek to attract a partner and the kind of interaction that we are likely to encounter. She is related to *eros*, which projects itself as our psychic desire for connections and relationship. Venus in our birth chart also represents how we need to transform our emotional and relationship values.

A dynamically aspected Venus in our chart may indicate that we are excessively attached to appearances, physical comfort, and emotional satisfaction. However, in its highest symbolic context, Venus may manifest in devotional practices and self-sacrificing service. The appreciation of the fleeting is transmuted into an awareness of real beauty and impersonal love.

Mars

The Power of Volition
Ruler of Aries

Mars is the archetype of assertiveness, force, and change.

Let the battle rage,
For victory is certain.
Standing strong with vision clear,
I am the Sublime Warrior.

Mars corresponds to the high-spirited hero within us all. He symbolizes the self-will of our ego as it seeks dominance over the physical and psychic resources of our environment. This primal initiatory force within us radiates tremendous power, incisiveness, vitality, and dynamic action. It symbolizes our capacity for endurance, strength, and courage.

Mars is male sexual potency. Assertive and forceful in achieving its desires, Mars brooks no interference from others. Mars is the primal warrior, determined to go through life battling courageously and prepared to die in the crusade of whatever is deemed to be righteous. Mythologically, Mars has always been connected with war and aggression. The red planet was called *Nergal* by the Babylonians and governed pestilence, fire, heat, and blood. The Romans called Mars *Ares*, the warrior-god.

Mars is the polar opposite of Venus. While Venus seeks the integration of diverse factors and a harmonious result, Mars desires change and challenge. He represents an inability to work within the prevailing family, social, or political environment. This inability to fit in and compromise naturally results in a violent clash of wills and, ultimately, open conflict prevails.

In our birth chart Mars symbolizes our capacity to take courageous pioneering action. Mars also reveals how our anger buttons are pushed and how we are likely to deal with the competitive nature of life. Mars indicates where we need to examine our desires and use of personal power. He forces us to confront our real motives and true desires. The lower manifestations of Mars range from anger, a constant turbulence of the emotional life and violence to antagonism, lust, and cruelty. Its higher manifestations include an indomitable will and the courage to take action for the benefit of others.

Jupiter
4

The Philosophical Benefactor
Ruler of Sagittarius

Jupiter is the archetype of optimism, opportunity, and expansion.

To all true seekers,
Come rewards of beneficence.
For riding high in sky chariot,
Is the great conciliator,
Our Lord of Fortune.

Mythologically, Jupiter was the king of the gods. As the Greek *Zeus* and the Roman *Jove* he radiates his sunny and beneficent nature to all. Jupiter is expansive and optimistic in stark contrast to fiery and assertive Mars. Jupiter sees a vision and with abundant social consciousness and optimism travels onwards, effortlessly drawing all things necessary for the manifestation of the vision.

Jupiter symbolizes growth opportunities that life presents to us, as well as our desire for freedom and movement—both mentally and physically. Jupiter also symbolizes a pronounced desire for a lack of restraint and a love of speculative, risky endeavors.

Jupiter is a future-oriented symbol. In our personal lives Jupiter opens the door to new plans, aspirations, and improvements and urges us towards growth, abundance, and free-spirited living.

The Jupiterian disposition displays an inherent lack of fear, restlessness, and a fundamental warmth. Jupiter calls us to seek philosophical expansions, new vistas in thought, and exciting geographical adventures. Jupiter is the great benefactor, the bestower of all good things. Fortunate in the extreme, this happy-go-lucky fellow dances through life with a joyful exuberance that mere mortals can only dream about.

In our birth chart Jupiter shows where we are too attached to doing things in a big way, where we overextend and go to excess in physical, emotional, mental, and spiritual ways. Jupiterian individuals are usually cheerful, generous, fair-minded, and jovial. However, overindulgence, a lack of humility, as well as exaggerated, extravagant, and wasteful behavior manifest as the excessive outpourings of Jupiter.

Saturn

♄

The Principle of Limitation
Ruler of Capricorn

Saturn is the archetype of structure, form, and stability.

Pathway initiator and teacher,
Leading us ever onwards.
Somber and quiet form builder,
Deep wisdom etched upon your brow.

Saturn correlates mythologically with the Greek god *Chronos,* "old man time" with his sickle, who metes out justice impartially and impersonally. Originally, he was connected with agriculture and dense metals but apparently lost his rulership over this domain due to his foul temper and evil ways. So vile was his temperament that he is said to have devoured all of his children except Zeus, who eventually conquered him.

As the complement of Jupiter, Saturn represents restriction, caution, responsibility, limitation, and austerity. Saturn contracts where Jupiter expands, Saturn is depressive and inhibited while Jupiter is manic and extroverted.

In our birth chart Saturn symbolizes our capacity for intense focus, self-sacrifice, patience, and hard work. In its more difficult manifestations Saturn symbolizes our fears, insecurities, anxieties, guilt, and other self-limiting paradigms that we have built into our consciousness. Saturn manifests as authoritarian, controlling, serious, humorless, dogmatic, rigid, conservative, and ill-natured temperaments.

As the personification of age and experience, Saturn symbolizes the austere teacher who methodically guides us through life's difficult lessons. As the harsh and exacting taskmaster, Saturn solidifies our inner psychic structures and causes crystallization of our old patterns of life and personality. Saturn demands that we take a realistic approach to life. We are forced to learn our hard lessons by delays, disappointments, and setbacks. Saturn shows us where we are too attached to social norms and approval and where we value power, authority, and reputation excessively.

Saturn in our birth chart reveals where we seek security through demonstrating tangible results and shows in what specific area of our life we are most severely tested. In its highest sense, Saturn symbolizes how we can manifest our inner potential by steadfastly destroying and creating new forms. Saturnian experience is all about facing the harsh lessons of the physical plane life, learning about our limitations. If we are wise we learn to accept our difficult life experiences and embrace our present circumstances. In doing so, we assimilate the ultimate Saturnian lessons of humility, modesty, wisdom, and understanding.

Uranus

The Illuminator
Ruler of Aquarius

Uranus is the archetype of revolutionary change, liberation, and originality.

Uranus the radical, clear and strong,
Willful messenger from unknown galaxies,
A clarion call, a loud and triumphant prayer.

Uranus is the first of three trans-Saturnian planets. These planets lead us out of our old patterns of being. They guide us towards expressing a new individual and social consciousness.

Mythologically, Uranus relates to *Ouranos*, primeval god of the universe. He was the son of Mother Earth and the father of the Titans, who later castrated him. Interestingly, Uranus correlates to bisexuality, homosexuality, and other unconventional sexual expressions. Uranus can also be linked to Prometheus, who stole fire from the gods and in so doing enabled humans to extend the reach of their knowledge.

Uranian energy destroys the rigidly structured Saturnian forms with a violence and willfulness that leaves total destruction in its wake. The psychological and spiritual ramifications of Uranian upheaval are tremendous, but understandably most of us are unable to fully grasp its full significance while we are still in the midst of Uranian inner tumult and catharsis.

Uranus symbolizes our desire to indulge in radical and unacceptable social behavior and represents our more perverse desires and inclinations. Uranus governs reformation, humanitarianism, eccentricity, inventiveness, as well as electrical, magnetic, and atomic forces.

As the awakener, Uranus operates at the subliminal levels of our higher mind. He symbolizes forces and processes that manifest as flashes of insight, intuition, sudden changes in our life pattern, highly original and innovative ideas, inventions, as well as rebellious, independent, unconventional, brilliant, and erratic behavior. In all these ways Uranus seeks to extend our rational thought processes and lead us toward an attunement (be it unstable and erratic) to Universal Mind where all polarities merge in the unified intelligence of the One.

In our birth chart Uranus symbolizes the most highly stimulated areas of our life. Uranus stirs our inner and outer life with such intensity that we get strung-out, hyped-up, and restless for excitement, change, and adventure. We experience an electrification of these areas of life. In its highest context, Uranus indicates those parts of us that are being prepared for liberation and illumination.

Neptune

♆

The Power of Redemption and Surrender
Ruler of Pisces

Neptune is the archetype of dissolution and universality.

Great waters of life
Bearing all things,
Deep and inspiring bliss,
Merging all in All.

Mythologically, Neptune is the Roman version of the Greek god *Poseidon*. Poseidon carries a three-pronged trident and has dominion over the sea. Metaphysically, the sea symbolizes the primordial substance (the *anima mundi*, the soul of all things) out of which everything is created and ultimately to which everything will be reabsorbed.

Neptune dissolves the remnants that Uranus leaves upon its path of destruction. Slowly, but surely, we are shaken out of the stupor of materialism and led into realms of superphysical existence. Neptunian forces operate in ways that are absolutely beyond our conscious control; they are totally incomprehensible to our intellect. In order to respond positively to the Neptunian vibration we need to learn to surrender to it and allow ourselves to be led along a path of beauty, mysticism, inspiration, and spiritual union.

To journey safely through the sea of Neptunian forces we need to be well grounded, having learned the lessons of Saturn. For a premature openness and influx of the unconscious waters of life can be as destructive to psychological integration as it can be illuminating when we are properly prepared for the experience.

In psychological terms Neptune correlates to the boundless and formless collective unconscious. Neptune brings strange and unfathomable psychic experiences, weird dreams and fantasies, peak experiences, illusions, delusions, escapist tendencies, and direct experience of immaterial states. Neptune is a great melting pot of psychic debris for both the individual and the collective and brings to the surface the obscure contents of our unconscious mind.

As a higher octave of Venus, inspirational Neptune is a refiner of ideals. Neptune tantalizes us with visions of the ideal partner, ideal society, and ideal form—any ideal that will distract us from facing the harsh reality of our vulnerable and ephemeral earthly existence.

Neptune engenders exquisite artistic refinement and sensitivity by allowing us access to the immaterial and intangible realms of creation where dreams become realities.

In its highest symbolical context, Neptune indicates our capacity for forgiveness, impersonal love, and compassion. If our desire is strong enough, Neptune will guide us upon our spiritual voyage of self-discovery. Ultimately, Neptune will unveil all the mysteries of existence and show us how our senses have created a phantasmagoria upon which we have erroneously structured our lives.

Pluto

The Subterranean Destroyer
Ruler of Scorpio

Pluto is the archetype of regeneration, transmutation, and transfiguration.

> *Change perpetual, root and cause,*
> *A serpent's eternal testing time,*
> *Life and death, one and the same,*
> *The Self, unborn undying IS.*

Mythologically, Pluto was *Hades*, the god of the Underworld. Pluto symbolizes an intensely concentrated, ruthless, and seemingly cruel power. Plutonian forces are absolutely shocking in their consequences and secretive in operation. Pluto rules over the processes of regeneration, healing, elimination, life and death, and powerful sexual and emotional intimacy.

There is an inevitability and an unfathomable quality to Plutonian life processes. The changes wrought by this energy are drastic mind-blowing life developments that totally throw us out of our comfort zone into the unknown and the unknowable. Under Pluto's influence we are forced to let go of the things we hold near and dear. Pluto destroys all our erroneous physical, emotional, and mental attachments. Attachments are brutally shown for what they are.

The position of Pluto in our birth chart symbolizes either our tendency towards deep emotional attachments such as possessiveness, jealousy, and guilt, or our capacity to let go of negative psychic patterns and transmute ourselves into a more beautiful image of our Sacred Self.

The inscrutable Plutonian energy operates psychologically as obsessive, compulsive desires and drives. This energy can manifest as psychotic and violent behavior or just as easily be transmuted into more wholesome manifestations. Pluto is said to be a higher octave of Mars, but Pluto is inherently self-inhibited whereas Mars is self-projective. The overtly assertive energy manifestations of Mars are, in Pluto, transmuted into volcanic eruptions that cause physical and psychic devastation. The power of Pluto leaves everyone in its path running for cover.

Pluto, like Uranus and Neptune, symbolizes a transcendental force that causes the annihilation and absolute cessation of our old life processes, while at the same time it carries a promise of new and vital life potential. The transfiguration and resurrection of individuality symbolized by Pluto can only take place upon the death of the old personality structure. Pluto brings about a freedom from bondage for the individualized spirit; it's the phoenix rising from the ashes, the soul ascending to heaven.

6

The Ascendant
and the Houses

Each Sun is a thought of God and each planet a mode of that thought.

—Hermes

The *ascendant* is the name given to the sign of the zodiac that rises over the eastern horizon at the time and place of our birth. While our Sun sign is determined by the yearly cycle of the Sun through the heavens, our ascendant is determined by the cycle of the day, thus by Earth's rotation on its axis.

The circle surrounding our birth chart symbolizes the ecliptic, which is the apparent path of the Sun through the heavens. The horizon is represented by a horizontal line drawn through the circle. Our ascending degree becomes the cusp, or beginning, of our first house. It rises over the eastern horizon at the time of our birth. Quite naturally, the ascendant is often referred to as our rising sign.

Our birth chart has four ultrasensitive points called the *angles*: the ascendant; its opposing western point, the *descendant*; the southern point, called the *midheaven* ("MC"); and the northernmost point, the *imum coeli* ("IC"). The four angles mark the cusps or beginning of our first, seventh, tenth, and fourth houses, respectively. They form the backbone of our birth chart.

While the ascendant is generally considered to be, by far, the most sensitive angle in our birth chart, all of them are important as they correlate to foundational areas of our life. The angular houses—the first, fourth, seventh, and tenth—symbolize the identifying and determining factors in our life, namely, our self-expression and sense of personal identity, our home and family life, our relationship structures, and our career pathway.

Once our ascendant has been determined (computer software does it in about a second), the twelve houses of the birth chart follow sequentially from it (figure 2). The houses are experiential domains where the planets symbolically act and interact. Each house represents a specific dimension of our life experience. A house exhibits sensitivity to any planetary or zodiacal forces that are deposited in or found on the cusp of the house.

Our ascendant and the twelve houses set the boundaries of the archetypal potentiality symbolized by our planetary and zodiacal configuration at birth. They are the final determinants necessary to fully access our life pattern.

Spontaneous and Free Self-Expression

As previously noted, we are born in a moment of time, at a particular place, because the all-encompassing harmony and wisdom of the universe deemed that we fulfill a specific need of that moment, and that the "need of the moment" carries within itself both the fulfillment of the need and its essential spiritual meaning. In a very real sense our ascendant is a clear symbol of personal spiritual meaning.

To those sensitive to this energy, it's felt as a spontaneous inrush of dynamic vitality. The ascendant symbolizes our most natural way of self-expression. More than any other influence, including our Sun sign, the ascendant (and its major aspects) represents our most natural mode of self-projection. It is, at its core, the way our essential Selfhood (our Sun sign) seeks to relate to the world at large. The ascendant is, therefore, our vehicle of relating.

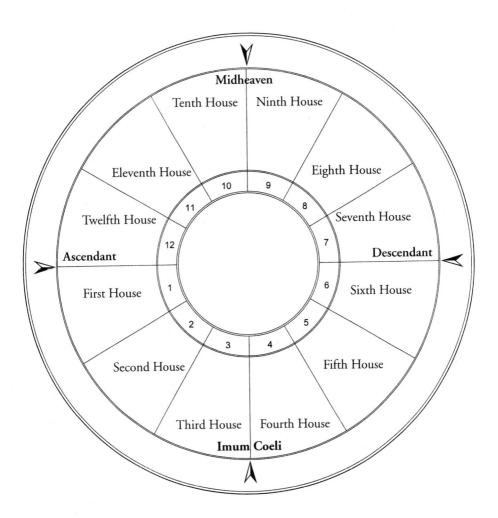

Figure 2. The Four Angles and the Twelve Houses

The ascendant not only symbolizes the way in which we seek to relate to others in a free and spontaneous way, but also symbolizes our physical body and has a lot to do with our general state of health. Moreover, any transits or progressions to our ascendant can affect our vitality and health—often quite dramatically.

Major transits to our ascendant, especially those of the trans-Saturnian planets, are indicative of critical life developmental phases—those great transitional moments when we seek to reinvent ourselves—sometimes by developing a new image, or more radically by building a whole new life.

This introduces another important concept relating to the ascendant—the ascendant symbolizes the mask that we wear. The ascendant is often symbolic of an image of personality that we project—our persona. The projected image is, more often than not, at variance with our innermost nature.

The ascendant tends to express itself along the lines of the element involved. For example: a fire-sign rising person will radiate an assertive, forceful, and ego-orientated persona, while an earth-sign rising person will be stable, practical, and capable in self-projection. An air-sign rising person will demonstrate adaptability, gregariousness, and spontaneity, while a water-sign rising person will exhibit strong feelings, sensitivity, and self-protective behavior. However, it's worth keeping in mind when interpreting the ascendant that a planet is a far more concentrated symbol of energy than a sign, so if a planet is strongly aspecting or conjunct our ascendant or in the first house, then the self-expression, image, or persona symbolized by the ascendant will be modified in line with the characteristic nature of the planet involved. Rising planets, whether situated in our first or twelfth houses, nearly always indicate major modification, strengthening, or coloring of our rising-sign temperament.

The Twelve Houses

A comprehensive analysis of your house meanings is dependent upon knowing precisely what planets fall into the various houses of your birth chart and, furthermore, what aspects the planets make.

Nonetheless, the following descriptions and lessons of the houses will aid you in developing an understanding of the astrological houses.

The First House

The first house is the house of personal identity and represents our personality and physical body. The individuality of our solar self is focused through the first house. Planets in our first house symbolize our level of independence, confidence, and spontaneity. A person with prominent first-house planets is likely to manifest an abundance of vitality, personal magnetism, and power.

The key meaning of first house planets is that they propel us towards initiating action in order to establish a more powerful or dynamic personal identity.

The tests of first-house planets are in the control of our ego. If your first house is overactivated, then it's likely that humility, modesty, selflessness, and self-control need to be cultivated.

The Second House

The second house symbolizes our values and security needs and rules over money, possessions, and wealth. It encourages practical and stable life experiences. Planets in our second house teach us to plan, to demonstrate consistency, and to seek wholesome and lasting values.

The key meaning of planets in our second house is that they operate in our lives by testing our capacity to manifest and use resources wisely. They indicate our need to maintain a secure material base.

The test of second-house planets is to use resources wisely for the benefit of the greater whole and not merely to satisfy our sensual or materialistic cravings. If you have a strong placement of planets in your second house you may need to develop greater honesty, transparency, and generosity with sharing yourself and your resources. The key concept is guardianship as opposed to personal ownership.

The Third House

The third house represents our urge for social and intellectual stimulus and sparks our desire for all kinds of communication. The third house is symbolic of analytical mind and rules over learning, speech, and perception. Third-house planets in our birth chart teach us to demonstrate greater openness, variety, adaptability, and versatility in our lives.

The key meaning of planets found in our third house is that they ask us to exhibit a greater degree of integration and mastery in our social and intellectual communication and learning skills.

Some of the tests for people with third-house planets revolve around their need to develop a more balanced approach to life. They may need to learn to feed their souls—to seek real and meaningful interchanges with others, as well as feeding their minds.

The tendency towards a lightweight intellectual approach to life needs to be guarded against, for third-house planets can stimulate an almost insatiable craving for exciting new things and ideas. The scattered and jangled nerves of the third-house type of individual need to be placated with poise and peace.

The Fourth House

The fourth house symbolizes our desire and need for a secure, safe, and protective home base for our activities. It represents a womb for our inner psychic life in which we seek to nurture, nourish, and care for ourselves and others. Planets in our fourth house unconsciously drive us towards a kind of psychological retreat, which will allow us to explore not only our deepest psychological needs, but also our family, cultural, and national roots.

The key meaning of planets found in our fourth house is that they symbolize a need for us to become involved in seeking peace and poise in our emotional life. They ask us to act in ways which will result in greater psychological integration at our deepest instinctive and emotional level.

The tests of fourth-house planets center upon us being overly self-protective, reclusive, cautious, morbidly sensitive, and melancholic. If you have planets in your fourth house you may need to develop a greater sense of fun, vitality, exuberance, and joy. Try moving out of your comfort zone and take a few risks in life.

The Fifth House

The fifth house encourages a dramatic extroversion of our individuality. It prompts us to build a more secure personal identity. The fifth house rules over children, romance, speculation, theatrical and dramatic displays, love affairs, and all kinds of recreation. Planets in our fifth house teach us to demonstrate new levels of confidence and creativity in our personal and social lives.

The key meaning of planets in our fifth house is that they ask us to project ourselves into life, to set an example, to lead, to create, to take calculated risks, and to think big. Fifth-house planets can indicate a bold and brazen approach to living that hides all kinds of inner insecurities, fears, and weaknesses. There can be an overemphasis on ego which compensates for an inner emptiness, insecurity, and lack of deep soul contact.

If you have many fifth-house planets, you may need to develop a service-oriented approach to others, and a more modest approach to yourself. The deep insecurities that are veiled by many fifth-house planets cannot be overcome by big displays, bravado, excessive generosity, or childlike dramatics. Nor are they completely hidden by romantic interludes or fun, games, and frivolity. Only sustained inner reflection and strenuous psycho-spiritual transformative therapy can lead us towards experiencing our true identity.

The Sixth House

The sixth house symbolizes our need to establish stable work habits and wise physical health regimes. It is traditionally related to service and employment. Fundamental to our overall health is not only appropriate diet and moderate exercise, but our capacity to purify the excesses of our ego-dominated self-expression, as represented by the fifth house.

The sixth house rules employment, sickness, health, diet, and work. Planets in our sixth house indicate in what ways we analyze and discipline ourselves. They suggest that it is time to eliminate the nonessential so that equilibrium, purity, and clarity can be established in our life. The reevaluation of emotional and mental patterns symbolized by planets in this house allows us to slowly and methodically transmute our old patterns into something more useful and lasting. Neurotic, overly fastidious, petty, and prudish behavior are some of the manifestations seen when a person overemphasizes the details of life while losing sight of the whole.

One of the key meanings of planets in our sixth house is that they symbolize our need to be discriminating over the right use of our physical, emotional, and mental resources.

The tests of the sixth house involve us accepting the need for sustained work and discipline. Through prolonged work, patience, practice, and trial we learn the lessons of the sixth house, which involve taking care of ourselves and others in wholesome, life-enhancing ways. This becomes our expression of real service.

The Seventh House

The seventh house symbolizes our need for partnership and our desire for social unity. Planets in our seventh house show in what way we relate to others through intimate one-on-one encounters, specifically, marriage but also business relationships. The seventh house rules over our social conscience and our urge to collaborate, share, and exchange views with others.

The kinds of relationships symbolized by planets in our seventh house are usually structured and legally binding arrangements and agreements that involve us in joint responsibilities, duties, self-sacrifice, and limitations. Fifth-house relationships, on the other hand, are more likely to be playful affairs, friendships, or fun, romantic interludes.

The key lesson that goes with planets in our seventh house is that through a committed relationship we learn to share at a deep and meaningful level with another human being.

The tests of the seventh house involve our capacity for compromise, thoughtful behavior, social responsibility, and honesty. Seventh-house planets can test us severely as the reality of the permanence and lack of freedom of a committed relationship makes itself felt.

Planets in our seventh house teach us to reassess our desire and compulsive drive for relationships so that ultimately we may attract relationships that express a degree of love and harmony that is conducive to our physical emotional, mental, and spiritual well-being.

The Eighth House

The eighth house symbolizes our desire to find security at the level of our deepest feelings and instinctual needs. If you have many planets in your eighth house your life may be like a battlefield where the forces of transformation bring about the end of old cycles of life and the birth of new ones. The eighth house traditionally rules over the processes of elimination, joint resources, investments, legacies, insurance, corporations, sex, death, and rebirth.

Planets in your eighth house symbolize huge opportunities for inner growth through surmounting the most severely testing life experiences. They represent our capacity to refine and redefine our whole personality structure. They drive us in search of real meaning in our lives. These planetary positions also correlate with a very thorough and persistent way of getting things done.

The negative manifestations of eighth-house planets can be quite drastic. They include psychotic, violent, ruthless, devious, manipulative, and sexually perverse behavior.

The key meaning of the eighth house is that we all have an incredible power at our disposal to make transformations both in our own psychic nature and in the lives of others.

The tests of our eighth house involve the use of personal power, that is, how we use our emotional, mental, and sexual energies. On a lower arc of manifestation, there can be an excessive focus on ego and on manipulative and demanding behavior. If you have many planets in your eighth house you may need to lighten up and manifest more joy, trust, and openness in your life.

The Ninth House

The ninth house symbolizes how we learn through refining and developing our abstract reasoning and intellectual faculties. Planets in this house represent our desire to set goals, manifest ideas, be well educated, and socially adept. Traditionally, the ninth house rules over higher learning, law, publishing, long-distance travel, sports, future-orientated activities, dreams, prophecies, philosophy, metaphysics, and religion.

The key meaning of planets in our ninth house is that by expressing strong beliefs and ideals we can manifest a consistent and exuberant joyousness and vitality in our lives.

Planets in our ninth house symbolize our ability to expand ourselves through ongoing study, reading, religious, and metaphysical pursuits. The faults symbolized by planets in this house include a dogmatic, arrogant, and flawed approach to seeking.

The tests of our ninth house planets are centered upon us not only thinking about, but demonstrating idealism and spirituality in our lives. If you have many ninth-house planets you may need to live fully in the here and now and not seek escapism in the form of dreams, visions, and causes which merely feed your attachment to egocentric ways of being.

The Tenth House

The tenth house symbolizes our career and outer attainments, as well as how we wield power and adapt to authority. It is an experiential domain where we take strenuous action to play our part in society. The tenth house seeks to thoroughly inculcate us with the work ethic—it asks us to demonstrate tangible results.

Planets in our tenth house propel us towards achieving our worldly ambitions. Traditionally, the tenth house rules over fame, power, our profession and career, our father or other authority figures, the state, and large-scale organizations. Planets in our tenth house correlate with an ambitious and determined attitude towards worldly achievement. If you have many tenth-house planets you may be unconsciously driven to reach career goals.

The key meaning of planets in our tenth house is that they symbolize opportunities for us to develop and demonstrate, on the world stage, our talents in a practical and rigorous manner so that we can build a secure future for ourselves and our families.

The tests of the tenth house involve an unbalanced and overly ambitious ego that pursues success and achievement at all costs. If your tenth house is overstimulated you may be too attached to recognition, to accomplishment, and to your personal power and reputation.

The Eleventh House

The eleventh house symbolizes our need for increased social involvement, acceptance, and responsibility. Planets in this house incline us towards communicating and learning by experiencing interpersonal relationships, whether one-on-one friendships or group involvement and activities.

If you have an eleventh-house emphasis you will learn how to merge effortlessly into a group situation. Potentially, you can experience a new level of personal freedom, purpose, uniqueness, and security by doing so. The eleventh house rules over friends, groups, clubs, societies, and was traditionally called the "house of hopes and wishes."

The key meaning of planets in our eleventh house is that they symbolize that we all need an anchor and purpose for our endeavors outside of our family and career. Furthermore, by sharing and participating with others in achieving common objectives we develop tolerance, impersonal love, and a humanitarian spirit.

The tests of the eleventh house, like the fifth, involve subduing our ego in pursuit of the good of the group and working harmoniously with others to manifest a chosen ideal, vision, or goal. Another test involves learning that collective transformation can only come about through each of us individually repolarizing our personal creative energies so that we harmoniously synchronize with the collective social need.

The Twelfth House

The twelfth house is the house in which we learn about our deepest emotional and spiritual nature. We seek time to nurture our soul's development. The twelfth house symbolizes either our capacity for loving service, or our tendency towards escapism, neuroses, and repression.

The twelfth house traditionally rules over hospitals, prisons, asylums, unseen forces and enemies, the mystical, and the psychic. Planets in our twelfth house sensitize us to the subtle realities and currents of life. They may indicate a beauty of spirit that has learned the lessons of self-forgetfulness, compassion, and impersonal love.

The key meaning of planets in our twelfth house is that they symbolize our capacity to dissolve, transcend, or transmute patterns of behavior. They are indicative of our potential to spiritualize our lives with vital and meaningful interests, whether artistic, musical, religious, or spiritual.

The tests of the twelfth house involve leaving behind the tried and trusted pathways, and venturing into unknown and mysterious realms. A twelfth-house emphasis can symbolize deluded or escapist behavior, irrational fears, phobias, and insecurities, but it can just as easily symbolize a beautiful soul who effortlessly radiates a purity, strength, intelligence, and understanding that is not of this world.

Table 7. The Twelve Houses

House	Meaning
I	The self, personality, vitality, self-projection, and the physical body
II	Personal resources, security needs, values, and income
III	Intellectual pursuits, brothers, sisters, short journeys, communication, speech, perception, and books
IV	Home environment, mother, instinctive feelings, traditions, and early life
V	Personal expression, creativity, children, love life, speculation, and games
VI	Work, health, service, apprentice, employment, duties, and diet
VII	Partnerships and marriage
VIII	Joint resources, inheritances, renewal, death, transformation, sex, and psychological complexes
IX	Higher education, travel, metaphysics, religion, sport, law, goals, and the future
X	Career, father, reputation, ambition, authority, the state, and organizations
XI	Friendship, hopes, group activities, humanitarian pursuits, and inventions
XII	The inner life, seclusion, retreat, escapism, idealism, drugs, hospitals, confinement, and the mystical

7

Aspects of Sacred Change

Pear seeds grow into pear trees,
nut seeds grow into nut trees:
God seeds into God.

—Meister Eckhart

The planetary aspects in our birth chart symbolize the complexity of our psychology, the level of integration of our psycho-spiritual nature, and the kinds of archetypal tests and confrontations that we are likely to encounter upon our pathway. The astrology of self-empowerment primarily uses a number of aspects which are called the dynamic aspects. The most powerful dynamic aspects to work with are the square (90 degrees; symbol is □), the conjunction (0 degrees; symbol is ☌), and the opposition (180 degrees; symbol is ☍).

There are numerous other aspects, including dynamic aspects, such as the semi-sextile (30 degrees; symbol is ⊻), the sesquiquadrate (135 degrees; symbol is ⬓), and the quincunx (150 degrees; symbol is ⚻), as well as flowing aspects, which include the trine (120 degrees; symbol is △) and the sextile (60 degrees; symbol is ⚹).

In the exercises and therapies that follow we will predominantly focus on using the symbolism of the dynamic aspects as a key to inner transformation. It isn't that the flowing aspects are not an integral part of the birth chart (they are), but simply that the dynamic aspects are indicative of emotional and mental blockages that are nearly always problematical, so much so that they usually need to be worked with strenuously in order to affect positive changes in our lives.

Calling Forth the Hero Within

The dynamic aspects in our birth chart indicate where we need to confront our psychological limitations and blockages. More often than not, the dynamic aspects force us to develop a more refined approach to the area of life symbolized. This confrontation with our erroneous mental and emotional patterns, and the resultant inner tension, is often incredibly hard to bear. As always, the greater the tension the greater the psycho-spiritual growth potential. As Carl Jung dryly stated, "There is no coming to consciousness without pain."

The dynamic aspects in our birth chart nearly always indicate both inner and outer conflicts that we cannot help but encounter. Events and situations subtly or not so subtly envelop us. We find ourselves in circumstances that, consciously at least, we would have tried hard to avoid at any cost. These situations and circumstances are evidently staged to bring to the surface of our consciousness past psychic residue that's ripe for transmutation. The inner tension and growth potential inherent in these difficult life situations, combined with the pain we experience, impel the brave amongst us to call forth the spirit hero within. If we have sufficient inner stillness and a clear awareness we may intuit that the forces of sacred change are upon us.

Most of us realize that our past psychic debris (our mental and emotional baggage) needs to be transmuted in order for self-empowerment and personal unfolding to transpire. Unfortunately, many of us still lean towards manifesting a degree of avoidance and repression. We try to convince ourselves that our problems will go away or somehow resolve themselves. Sometimes we try to repress or ignore them completely. In both these instances we are definitely in psycho-spiritual denial.

It's only natural for us to want to maintain a degree of control in our lives. Most of us like to feel as if we have our hands firmly on the reins of our destiny. However, our ingrained tendency towards avoidance, denial, repression, and seeking control is absolutely inimical to inner growth and self-empowerment.

In order to use positively and effectively the techniques outlined in this book, we need to let go of our desire to be in control. After all, at the level of our personality and ego we are incredibly vulnerable and fragile. We are definitely not in control. This is the reality of our existence.

We need to learn to trust our inner process implicitly. In order to do this we need to trust ourselves and others. Ultimately, we need to trust in life. Without this simple trust and faith in the goodness of life all techniques and methods of personal development are doomed to failure for we would fall at the first hurdle.

Aspects of Grace

The dynamic aspects in our birth chart, particularly when they are catalyzed into activity by major transits of Uranus, Neptune, and Pluto, beat down upon us with chthonic power. Under these circumstances, any form of avoidance, denial, or repression is not a wise option: at best, it is a temporary palliative; at worst, it represents an emotional and mental contraction that inevitably leads to all kinds of neuroses.

It's critical that we confront head-on the issues symbolized by our dynamic aspects. If we don't face the lessons indicated then life will tend to throw more unpleasant experiences our way in the form of illness (emotional, mental, and physical) or severe outer crises until eventually we are abruptly catapulted out of our old ways.

The great inner currents of life—the unconscious and the superphysical—cannot be checked by willpower alone, nor can they be ignored for long without tragic consequences. In reality it's our Higher Self who has called forth the lesson, the crisis, and all it entails.

As we have seen, the dynamic aspects in our birth chart indicate deep-seated patterns of behavior and overriding tendencies in our psychological nature. They usually manifest as compulsive and unconscious modes of self-expression. As we move through the unfolding cycles of our life we will naturally encounter many different kinds of experience—the highs and lows of living. Our traumatic experiences illumine and refine our perception of "who we really are." They clarify the part we are to play in the drama of creation. Dynamic aspects are sacred symbols of opportunity. They allow us, if we are brave, to take a quantum leap in our evolutionary journey. They are, in the final analysis, aspects of grace.

Aspects of Empowerment

The planetary aspects in our birth chart symbolize the intricacy and complexity of the psychological dynamic that operates within us. In practice, aspects are calculated in degrees along the circle of the ecliptic (figure 3). Lines are drawn from Earth to two planets and a measurement of the angle or arc formed is taken. An aspect doesn't have to be exact to be effectual. An orb or allowance out of exactness is acceptable in the calculation of aspects. The major aspects used in astrology are listed below:

Table 8. The Aspects

Symbol	Name	Degrees	Orb
☌	Conjunction	0°	10°
⌵	Semi-sextile	30°	2°
∠	Semi-square	45°	2°
✳	Sextile	60°	4°
Q	Quintile	72°	2°
□	Square	90°	10°
△	Trine	120°	8°
⊡	Sesquiquadrate	135°	3°
⊼	Quincunx	150°	3°
☍	Opposition	180°	10°

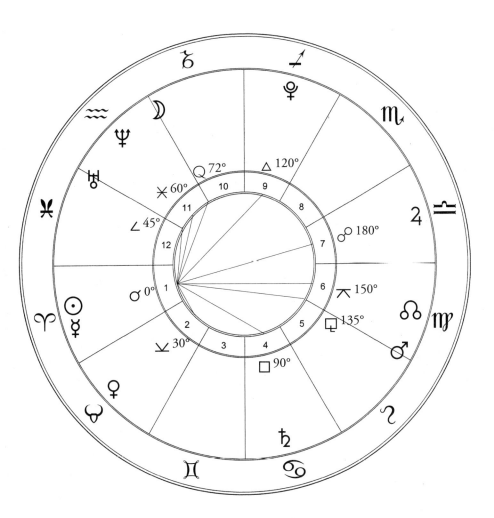

Figure 3. The Aspects

Aspects of Dynamic Energy and Adjustment

As we have seen, the dynamic aspects are the conjunction, square, opposition, sesquiquadrate, quincunx, and semi-sextile (see figure 3). These are the aspects, par excellence, of the astrology of self-empowerment for they encourage us to take action. They drive us towards inner growth and the actualization of our life potential in a way which isn't evident with the flowing aspects. Because of this factor, transformational astrology has always recognized that it's far more useful to use the dynamic aspects in therapeutic work.

When we work consciously with our dynamic aspects, we begin to take responsibility for our emotional and mental manifestations and our life circumstances. The challenges symbolized and encountered may be absolutely immense, but this is precisely the challenge necessary to bring out the best in us. If the challenge is faced courageously, we will successfully pass an important life test and a new level of personal integration is attained with its concomitant peace and joy.

Dynamic aspects challenge us to make dramatic adjustments in our approach to some part of our life. Such aspects focus our consciousness upon specific attachments, weaknesses, and deficiencies. Ultimately, they force a reversal of our energy flow. There can be no denying the enormous potential for personal unfolding from these aspects but, as always, the critical factors are our desire to trust the process, accept our predicament, and consciously participate in a life-enhancing way.

There are many ways that a particular aspect can manifest externally in our lives. The archetypal lesson may be clearly symbolized by the aspect, but the existential reality—the specific events or unique circumstance—can only be surmised.

Dynamic aspects always release energy. They challenge the status quo and propel us out of our comfort zone. Through encountering in a positive way our most difficult, traumatic, and painful experiences, we learn to let go of the past, and release the emotional and mental baggage we carry around. In the process we become more whole, more loving, and more compassionate human beings.

With all the dynamic aspects it's easy to lack objectivity and project our fears, attachments, anxieties, inhibitions, blockages, and inadequacies onto others. This particularly applies to the squares and oppositions but, to a lesser extent, it's true of all the dynamic aspects. Whatever the particular events and circumstances surrounding our dynamic aspects, one thing is certain: sooner or later the challenge symbolized must be encountered.

Aspects of Sacred Self-Discovery

A conjunction (☌) between two planets symbolizes a merging and intense interaction of the planetary energies. Any conjunction in our birth chart represents a major theme concerning the way in which we seek to project ourselves in the world. The energy release of a conjunction is normally clear and powerful. It represents a part of our psychological makeup that is pivotal to our individuality.

A square (□) between two planets is indicative of a tense and conflicting energy interaction. Squares test our ability to achieve integration and harmonious expression of the energies symbolized. They show where tension is built up and released, where we feel driven to take action, and where compulsive patterns of behavior and self-expression (or self-repression) operate in our lives.

An opposition (☍) between planets is also symptomatic of a problematical energy interaction. Relationship difficulties can be severe with these aspects. As with the squares, the capacity for inner tension and outer conflict is immense. As its name implies, an opposition symbolizes a part of our energy field that needs to be confronted head-on.

With some of the oppositions and squares we see manifestations of self-destructiveness, violence, and rage that are incredibly difficult to control, transmute, or channel positively. Like any pattern in consciousness, over time, with the right techniques, great progress can be made to refine the expression of the psychic force involved.

Personal and Trans-Saturnian Planetary Aspects

The Sun, the Moon, Mercury, Venus, and Mars are called the personal planets. They symbolize primary and personal parts of our individuality: our self-expression, emotions, mind, relationship capacity, will, and volition. On the other hand, the trans-Saturnian planets (Uranus, Neptune, and Pluto) symbolize an order of life and consciousness that is beyond the purely personal. The outer planets are more like transcendental, intergalactic messengers who come into our lives to act as catalysts to speed up our evolutionary process.

When a personal planet is in dynamic aspect with a trans-Saturnian planet we have a very important key to our unfolding symbolized. These aspects clearly indicate the need to transmute some major part of our energy field. The aspect should be worked with in combination with the prescribed techniques of affirmation, invocation, visualization, and crystal energy transformation.

Uranian Catharsis

Any personal planet in dynamic aspect to Uranus is extremely stimulated. Uranus, symbolically, shakes us out of our old patterns of living, usually in sudden, shocking, and dramatic ways. Uranian energy generates within us a powerful urge towards freedom and experimentation. It exponentially speeds up the natural rhythm of our lives.

These aspects symbolize the potential to totally repolarize our energy flow, make fundamental changes in our way of life and self-expression, leave the past behind, and experiment with new, exciting, and radical ways of living.

The Uranian force is absolutely unpredictable. It's capable of changing our reality, and our consciousness, in a split second. Any exercises or therapies involving Uranus will encourage sudden, unexpected, and fundamental changes to the area of life you are working on. Remember, Uranus breaks all of your and society's rules and conventions. So, when you work with Uranus, expect the unexpected.

Neptunian Dissolution and Emergence

Any dynamic aspect between your personal planets and Neptune symbolizes the potential for an opening of your consciousness into an order of life that is transpersonal and transcendental: an order of the Divine Life that is totally beyond the normal level of human experience. Neptune, unlike Uranus, dissolves our ego-dominated feelings and mental states.

Neptune leads us, slowly and inexorably, into realms of life that have no boundaries and no recognizable forms. When we are in the grip of a major Neptunian transformation our established perceptions of reality are totally stripped away; there is absolutely nothing left to cling to.

Neptune helps us to reformulate our life paradigms, but first comes the utter dissolution of the dross of the old personality structure. If letting go were easy, Neptunian dynamic aspects would be experienced with great joy and peace. Because we are attached to our psycho-spiritual patterns and states, to people, and environments, we will often experience a total disorientation, dislocation, mental miasma, and general confusion when Neptune (symbolically) takes hold of us.

If we learn to trust our inner process and lose our attachment to forms and feelings (at least temporarily) we can flow with Neptunian transformative energy more easily. Neptune, symbolically, frees us from all limitation, revivifies our imaginative faculties, and opens our inner psychic doorways. If you desire to unlock your latent creative power, attune to the mystical beauty of life, and experience directly the Oneness that is our true essence, then Neptune in dynamic aspect to any of your personal planets is a good place to start. Even if you have no dynamic aspects, work with Neptunian energy, anyway. Its blessings and bliss await you.

Plutonian Transfiguration

Any personal planet in dynamic aspect to Pluto provides us with amazing potential to channel power into transformative activities.

Pluto operates at the deepest and most unfathomable (almost subterranean) levels of our being. Out of "no-thing" Pluto emerges to force change upon us. Our deepest soul calls for freedom from bondage have been heard. Pluto is the "clarion call of the beyond" that comes to shatter and pulverize our old patterns. Pluto drags us, kicking and screaming, into a new cycle of life.

Plutonian energy operates on many different levels to affect sacred soul alchemy. If we invoke Plutonian power we should be prepared for mind-blowing events—a volcanic catharsis of monumental proportions. The dynamic personal planet aspects with Pluto allow for a generation of power and will that is capable of bringing about such positive change that it beggars our imagination. Plutonian energy should never be underestimated. Through the destruction of the acorn seed, the mighty oak establishes itself. Through the destruction of our seemingly weak and vulnerable personality structure, a towering spiritual being emerges. Pluto makes all things possible through the power of transmutation and transfiguration.

If you are prepared to travel to the depths of your inner nature in order to be reborn, then Pluto is ever ready to guide you through the process. Expect only to suffer the total rending of all that you hold near and dear. If you would claim your true birthright by working with the Plutonian forces then you must trust implicitly in the Higher Power. Only utter self-sacrifice, impersonal love, and pure compassion will suffice to guard you along the way. Pluto is only for the brave.

8

Astrological Affirmations and Invocations

When a blade of grass is cut the whole universe quivers.

—Upanishad

Throughout the ages the demonstration of the word, through spoken or silent affirmation, has been one of the great keys to personal transformation and the reclaiming of our sacred power. And so it remains.

The spoken word has a transformative power all of its own, but when combined with the language of the subconscious mind—symbol, suggestion, and visualization—it's lifted into the realm of the sublime as an amazing psychological regenerative tool.

In order to reclaim our power, achieve psychological integration, develop loving kindness, harmlessness, compassion, and lasting joy we must moment by moment demonstrate the word. In its highest and purest form, the word will express through you, and you through it, a complete and honest transparency in all your words and thoughts, and a purified and poised emotional expression together with a strength and beauty of spiritual force which seem almost incomprehensible to those not upon the way.

The spoken word can be used in many ways in the therapeutic arts. Two of the most efficacious techniques that can be directly related to the birth chart, and thus to astrological self-empowerment, are the techniques of affirmation and invocation. However, before we examine in more detail some planetary affirmations and invocations, let's look at the role our thoughts and subconscious mind play in creating our reality.

The Power of Our Thoughts

If we desire to change our lives we need to change the nature of the thoughts that we allow to impinge upon our consciousness moment by moment. The first step to reclaiming our power is to analyze the nature of our thought processes. We need to pay more attention to the quality and nature of our thoughts in order to change our circumstances.

You may like to try the following experiment. Simply note over a period of twenty-four hours the kinds of thoughts and feelings that run through your mind. Note your desires, fears, how you talk to yourself internally, the strength or weakness of your thoughts, etc. This list is very revealing and illuminating in itself. Few of us realize just how negative, trivial, deluded, unimaginative, uncreative, and facile our mental patterns have become. Upon analysis it's usually the case that even the most together of us score abysmally in this experiment.

It becomes clear, upon an examination of our birth chart, that there is a synchronicity between our thoughts and the potentiality indicated in the chart. If nothing more, our birth chart is a clear and concise map of the kinds of thoughts and emotions that we perennially entertain. The problem for most of us is that our inner creations get out of control and become our master instead of us directing our thoughts to build the reality we desire.

We build our reality not by single thoughts but by establishing habitual patterns of thought. These currents or themes in our thought-life become ingrained in our subconscious mind and take on a power of their own: power to heal; power to create disease; power to give courage or create fear; power to build prosperity or inflict poverty, and so on. Remember, our thoughts are always seeking manifestation through our physical, emotional, and mental expressions.

Powerful Thought Currents Create Potent Manifestations in Matter

A single thought usually has little power, but if it is repeated many times over several months, tremendous force is generated in our subconscious and conscious minds. This is the key to the use of affirmation and invocation techniques. By constant and prolonged repetition of affirmations, new positive patterns are created and negative ones dissipated. This is one of the most profound secrets of transmutation.

We don't have to shovel out the darkness of an old troublesome pattern. We simply turn on the light of the new and beautiful pattern we wish to supplant it with. A thousand living, dynamic thoughts that are affirmed with strong emotion will ignite within us a deep and stable new pattern capable of radically changing our lives.

Wise men and women from many cultures have, for centuries, used *mantras*, which are simply potent vibratory chants. A mantra (in Sanskrit, literally "an instrument of thought") is based upon the idea that there is a sacred seed sound underlying all creation, and that by the affirmation and repetition of the mantra we can ultimately have direct awareness of and communion with this primal creative sound.

Our Invisible Helper

Our subconscious mind is the mechanism by which the mixture of our thoughts and emotions take on physical manifestation in a seemingly magical way. It knows everything that has ever happened to us and records every image, smell, sensation, and sound that we have ever experienced. It's also the controlling center from which all our biological life processes and functions are directed.

Significantly, it's been discovered that our subconscious mind is always available to provide us with guidance, ideas, insights, and answers to our specific needs. This invisible helper and partner on our life journey is like our very own genie, except that rather than speaking directly to it and giving it instructions, we usually speak to it in obscure and subtle ways.

Celestial Affirmations Are Axiomatic Truths

Affirmation means different things to different people. However, in the context of Sacred Astrology, let's define it as meaning any combination of words that are said, aloud or silently, with great intent and breathed into life with strong psychic energy. The word, phrase, or statement conveys an intelligent truth relating to our individuality and our potentiality as symbolically encoded in our birth chart.

An astrological affirmation is stated as if it's an incontestable axiomatic truth of life not open to any of the reasoning dialectics of the rational mind. It's a statement of power related to what is already within us. In other words, we are not calling upon an outside force or person to aid us, but believe deeply that the meaning and truth contained in the affirmation is already a latent part of us.

Affirmation is one of the simplest techniques to use to influence our subconscious mind and to affect positive change in our lives. Because most of us can only hold one thought at a time, an affirmation is able to plant the seed in our consciousness of the desired outcome. Points to remember:

- Always affirm positively and be as precise as possible.

- Affirm daily.

- Affirm with great emotional intensity. In doing so, your affirmations will reap more rapid results.

- Short affirmations are easier to repeat and remember.

- Regularly affirm and acknowledge your successes—be gentle on yourself.

- Self-belief is the basis upon which we build our positive life manifestations. If you can't believe in yourself, try believing in your Self.

- Affirm that you are a unique person with amazing possibilities. This is nothing but the truth—your birth chart says as much. You are a *divine being* manifesting in time and space and have the right to draw abundance and joy into your life. The reality is that you have direct and unlimited access to the powerhouse of an abundant universe. Furthermore, you are a fragment of the totality of existence, an archetype born on Earth to fulfill a purpose and meet a need.

If you believe that the universe is just waiting to rally around to help you on your journey, unexpected and helpful things will happen to help you manifest your highest destiny. Events and circumstances will get behind you. You are (and will always be) supported by the abundance of the universal order.

Planetary Affirmations: Words of Power

Here are some planetary and zodiacal affirmations that can be used daily. You can use them individually or by combining two of them you can create a single affirmation that symbolizes an aspect or theme in your birth chart. You can also create your own aspect affirmations by using the key meanings of the planets or signs involved. (Examples are given later in this chapter on how to create your own person-centered aspect affirmations.)

☉ Affirmations for the Sun (and for Leo)

The universal power sustains me moment by moment.

I radiate my inherent and true Self with confidence.

I am a vital and dynamic person.

I am a center for the creative intelligence of life.

I am a beautiful and totally miraculous person in all ways.

Faith and hope are the cornerstones of my temperament.

I am affectionate and graciously receive affection from all.

I build a strong and healthy body day by day.

I receive Earth's abundance and generously give to all.

I am demonstrative and loving with my children.

I know how to play and enjoy myself.

I am a joyous person who inspires trust and confidence in others.

I am the vital principle of all that is.

☽ Affirmations for the Moon (and for Cancer)

I respond sensitively to the needs of others.

I care about myself and my children.

I build a supportive and protective family environment.

I am highly imaginative.

The Universal Mother dwells within me.

I trust my instincts.

I am ready to receive all of life's gifts.

My past is behind me, I reside in the present.

My feelings are pure and I respond positively to life.

I trust others and trust myself.

I embody Divine Love and so I forgive.

I lose sight of myself in service of others.

I am passive, patient, and tenacious.

The more I change the more stable I become.

I love and nurture all life.

☿ Affirmations for Mercury ♀ (and for Gemini and Virgo)

I am brilliant and clever to boot.

Scintillating intelligence pervades my aura.

I am so logical, logical, logical.

I speak in intelligent, melodious tones.

Universal mind is my essence.

I am incredibly versatile and oh-so perceptive.

I am curious, inquisitive, and expressive.

I analyze and see clearly all my patterns.

Wise thoughts stream out of my consciousness.

Quickly and effortlessly I adapt to the need of the moment.

My mind is part of the Mind.

My eloquence speaks for itself.

I am clear, impartial, and fair in my thinking.

♀ Affirmations for Venus (and for Taurus and Libra)

I am at peace with my life.

I relate harmoniously with everyone.

I create beauty in all my endeavors.

I am perfect even now.

I embody and radiate impersonal love for all.

Diplomacy and tact are my friends.

I bring people together in joyous unison.

Love is my strength.

I yield and by yielding grow stronger.

I am attached to the most beautiful One.

I feel for all life with compassion and sensitivity.

I am a gracious, gentle, and artistic person.

I am completely satisfied and at peace with life.

I am peace and am crowned by love.

The creativity of the One flows through me.

♂ Affirmations for Mars (and for Aries)

I am a pioneer and a leader.

The strength of the spiritual warrior is with me now.

I am passionate about living.

I react quickly and powerfully to every challenge.

Impulsive I may be, but my initial impulse is right.

I am not rude, I am direct and speak the truth.

I am pulsing with energy as I act in the drama of life.

I am sure and certain in all my undertakings.

I am empowered with force and courage.

I am energized, heated, and ready for action.

Ever victorious am I—of victory I am certain.

I dominate only myself so that I may serve.

I am always ready to begin again.

I am the hero in a moment of crisis.

24 Affirmations for Jupiter (and for Sagittarius)

I create a positive future in this moment.

The more I give, the more I receive.

My nature is jovial and happy.

I attract all good things.

My enthusiasm and optimism know no bounds.

From joy I come, in joy I live.

I bring good fortune to all I touch.

I feel abundance all around me. I am abundance.

I see no problems, only solutions.

My mind is sound and clear, my heart strong.

I grow and learn moment by moment, never do I stand still.

I have broad visions of a grand future for all.

I see only opportunities and more opportunities.

♄ Affirmations for Saturn (and for Capricorn)

I am loyal almost to the point of a fault.

I happily carry all my responsibilities as if they are nothing.

I endure and will always endure beyond all.

I am patient for I understand the nature of time.

I aspire only to inspire.

I am careful, practical, and responsible.

I respect the authority of the Mighty One.

I subdue and control only myself.

I am secure in my divinity.

I build beautiful forms to share with others.

I do not grow older, I just grow.

I am impartially just, and yet I forgive.

♅ Affirmations for Uranus (and for Aquarius)

I am a caring friend to all.

I am spontaneous and original.

My personality is magnetic and all-attractive.

I enjoy change and adventure.

I am fascinated by life and am fascinating.

My motives are pure and humanitarian.

I live in perfect freedom.

I love radical change and upheaval.

I am fully awakened in the most perfect spiritual consciousness.

I possess dynamic willpower.

I am a creative genius; ideas come to me effortlessly.

Amidst the storms of my life I am poised; my vision is clear.

I am pervaded with scintillating intelligence.

♆ Affirmations for Neptune (and for Pisces)

I feel for all life with pure compassion.

I am a spiritual being filled with light and love.

I have dreamed beautiful dreams; now I manifest them.

My imagination knows no bounds.

I draw forth from all I meet the vision of Oneness.

I am very forgiving.

The peace of the infinite pervades my life.

My essence is love.

I manifest clear thoughts and pure emotions.

I flow effortlessly with the positive currents of life.

I am content in all ways.

I am a wonderful and inspirational person.

I am incredibly artistic and creative.

♇ Affirmations for Pluto (and for Scorpio)

I am strong and powerful.

I destroy only to build more beautiful forms.

I am the most loyal of friends.

I always persevere to the very end.

I feel deeply and then I think.

I face this crisis with courage.

I am always ready to begin again.

I live life to the fullest.

I speak the truth.

I am a power for positive change.

I attract real relationships.

I purify myself day by day.

♈ Affirmations for Aries

I am the beginning of all beginnings.

I am the fire of cosmic mind.

I am the sublime and mighty warrior.

I will things to happen.

I embody the intelligent power of the life-force.

I am the pulsating radiance of new life.

The universal intelligence stands behind all my endeavors.

I am one with the Source of All Power.

I am one with the Doer of All; yet of myself I do nothing.

I adore the living breath in all creatures great and small.

♉ Affirmations for Taurus

My wisdom shines forth.

I stand poised amidst the crashing of worlds.

Nothing can resist me.

Power flows through me.

I become stronger moment by moment.

The strength of the living force is in me.

I am anchored deep into the earth.

I desire the highest good for all.

I am a wise guardian of the earth's resources.

I understand and fully embrace my human needs.

I calm and purify my emotions daily.

♊ Affirmations for Gemini

I keenly observe, I discover, I discriminate.

I am a part of the All-Knowing Mind.

I see beyond appearances to the core of reality.

I am connected with all that is.

I relate to all with pure intelligence.

I joyfully dance in the interplay of the worlds.

I am fascinated with the dynamic relatedness of the All.

I inhale the fragrant breath of the Divine Consciousness.

I am a great mediator and facilitator.

My intelligence grows daily.

♋ Affirmations for Cancer

I am one with the Great Mother.

Maternal to my core, I cannot help but radiate love.

I am sustained and nurtured by the Moon Goddess.

I live in the heart of all beings.

I am absorbed in the great sea of life.

My loving nature opens all doors.

I drink daily from the fountain of blissful waters.

Compassion and understanding fill my consciousness.

I protect and nourish all of life's children.

I touch with a tender hand.

♌ Affirmations for Leo

My radiance lights all the worlds.

Beneficence crowns me.

I stand supreme, the meekest of the meek.

I emanate power, will, and wisdom.

I am a prince(ss) of this world.

In the battle of life I am ever-victorious, incapable of defeat.

The creative power is a projection of my Self.

I dream of mortal adventures and awake in the palace of the king.

The Jewel of Eternity is in my heart of hearts.

The glory of the Eternal One radiates from my consciousness.

I conquer all the phantoms of ignorance and delusion in my life.

♍ Affirmations for Virgo

I am patient and strong enough to carry my burden.

I am grounded in goodness.

I live to serve. Service is my life.

I devote myself to living the life.

Daily, I learn the secrets of self-mastery.

I am dedicated to worshipping all life.

In deepest silence I perfect my life.

As I am tested, the gold of my soul is refined.

Through all of life's experiences I remain forever pure.

♎ Affirmations for Libra

I am eternally posed in perfect balance.

I hear sweet divine melodies.

I am the fruitful mother of all life.

The vision of true love pervades my life.

As the battle rages, love is my strength and solace.

I extend the hand of loving friendship to all.

Creative intelligence pervades me.

Celestial rubies and fine gold garland my pure being.

My emotions are poised and pure.

I attract loving and fulfilling relationships.

♏ Affirmations for Scorpio

I am one with the vital principle of all that is.

I am the doer and the actor in all life dramas.

I am ever-triumphant.

I consciously unite with the Primal Source of All.

I wear the robe of self-mastery and carry the sword of clear perception.

My body is the palace of the king.

My desires lead me to divine self-expression.

The One Life maintains me in all states and conditions.

I die only to live again.

I destroy and transmute only to build more beautiful forms.

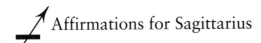 Affirmations for Sagittarius

The eternal sound whispers gently to me.

True vision takes hold of me.

I hear the clarion call of the great beyond.

I enter the sphere of true perception.

Throughout timeless ages I walk the great quest.

I am the illumined child of love and light.

I enjoy all my life adventures.

I am overwhelmed by joy and enthusiasm for living.

I vision a future of wholeness and goodness for all.

I fully accept my past and create an abundant future now.

♑ Affirmations for Capricorn

I embody the wisdom of the Mighty One.

Self-realization is upon me.

I never forget who I am.

I build wondrous forms.

I reflect the Light of the One in all my life's manifestations.

If I be lifted I will lift all others unto myself.

I shatter my outmoded crystallized forms.

I strive to daily embody generosity and thoughtfulness.

My work is fulfilling and meaningful.

Divine wisdom and understanding are with me now.

♒ Affirmations for Aquarius

The clear beauty of my wisdom shines.

I am ever free.

Though I experience manifold changes, I remain in essence unchanged.

The primal force of the divine idea manifests harmoniously in my life.

The wind of the Spirit moves over me.

I am an illumined child of earth and sky.

I am a transparent channel for the light of the worlds.

Liberation cascades upon me.

I support absolute freedom for all.

Limitless love and limitless truth are my essence.

♓ Affirmations for Pisces

I am a healing influence to all.

I dream magical and sublime dreams.

I am in all things; I am one with all life.

I am an image of divine perfection.

I existed before the worlds and I will always exist.

I am life eternal and the eternal longing for perfection.

The bliss of the universe pervades me.

I am a divine ripple upon the river of existence.

The conquest of delusion is complete.

I am filled with sublime compassion and forgiveness.

Explore Your Birth Chart Potential with Creative Affirmations

Pick an area of your life that you wish to change. It could be an area related to a house in your birth chart or a planet or a general theme of your life. Write down a list of what you feel is wrong with that area of your life. Be absolutely honest. When you have finished examine the list and look for erroneous beliefs or self-limiting affirmations that you habitually use. For example:

> *I just can't seem to have a permanent relationship.*

> *Men just end up using me.*

> *We always end up arguing.*

Next to each erroneous statement construct a new positive affirmation:

> *I build strong and stable relationships.*

> *I always attract men who respect me.*

> *My partner and I talk things through.*

Choose your new life-enhancing affirmation and begin the process of changing your reality. Remember that change is an ongoing and cumulative process. Our established patterns take time to change. It's never too late, but be patient and persevere.

Person-Centered Aspect Affirmations

Let's consider someone with the Sun conjunct Venus in his or her birth chart. We can construct a simple affirmation centered on the highest manifestation of this symbol by examining the symbol from its component parts and creating the affirmation as follows:

The Sun correlates to our life-force, our self-expression, and the energy and power that we have at our disposal. Venus correlates to our capacity to express relationship, love, and harmony, as well as to allow creative energy to flow in our life. In conjunction, this symbol in its higher octave correlates to a person who potentially can act as a pure channel for the artistic and creative forces of life, and who can express this through dynamic and harmonious relationships.

From this symbolic meaning we can construct many different affirmations. For example:

> *I am a pure channel for the creative love-energy of life.*

> *Harmony flows through me and by the birth of the love-force I am transformed.*

The possibilities of planetary aspect affirmations are endless. The important point is that an astrological affirmation relates directly to a powerful theme in your life. The significance of these astrologically constructed affirmations is that they relate directly to your energy field. Furthermore, if they are constructed using transits or progressions then they relate to a particular phase of development you are passing through. They are person-centered, uniquely made to fulfill a need. They can lead you through a crisis or vitalize some seed-potential that lies dormant within you.

Planetary and Zodiacal Invocation

In contrast to affirmation, invocation implies a calling forth of some power, energy, idea, or person that's part of the universal order. In reality there may be no difference between the "within" and the "without," but the dichotomy remains for all of us who haven't yet received the final beatitude of Self-realization. We perceive ourselves as being separate entities flowing in and through life, and that great life usually appears to us as something outside of ourselves.

Mystical literature states that everything is contained within us, and that when we reclaim this level of awareness—having always had it—the idea of a separate existence fades into the realm of fantasy and illusion. However, for our purposes the techniques of affirmation and invocation remain friendly and useful companions along our pathway towards self-empowerment.

Astrological invocation involves calling upon zodiacal and planetary archetypal energies. By doing so in a focused and potent way we draw them closer to us, and ultimately achieve the desired therapeutic outcome. Astrological invocation (like affirmation) is also personalized, but invocational statements are usually couched in the symbolic language of the particular planetary or zodiacal force invoked.

Planetary Invocations

Here are a few examples of some planetary invocations—one for each of the planets. Most of these invocations are nonspecific and invoke the symbolic power of the archetype but they can easily be tailored to your particular needs and desires. Experiment with the power of invocations and see your life transformed daily.

An Invocation of the Sun

Great Sun of Life, primal radiance, beloved of my heart, come and fill me with your vital force, warm loving touch, and indomitable strength. I desire your power, I invoke your creative spark, I call upon your abundance and joyousness to enter my life.

An Invocation of the Moon

I invoke the Goddess of the Waters, most adored one, primal and mythic protector of your children. I desire your nourishing and nurturing energy to fill the void within me. I need to feel your presence, I implore your loving force to come into my life.

An Invocation of Mercury

I invoke the sublime intelligence and true perception of Mercury. Fill me, my winged friend, with insight and clarity of mind. Shower upon me your dexterity of consciousness so that I may analyze and synthesize the manifold aspects of my life.

An Invocation of Venus

Beloved of my heart, dearest lover of all, Venus come to me now. I invoke your true and pure loving emotion to uplift and inspire me in all the ways of my life. Help me to express in ever greater measure the majestic love that creates and sustains all life. As I manifest your love I feel a joy and blessedness that is beyond words.

An Invocation of Mars

Come to me mighty warrior. I invoke the daring courage and power of Mars to enter my life. I feel your passion and strength. I call forth the spirit hero within myself to resonate with your energy. I am now vitalized with initiative, drive, and masculine force.

An Invocation of Jupiter

I invoke the beneficent power of Jupiter. I call forth your optimism and enthusiasm into my life. Help me to channel broad and abundant divine visions into the reality of my life. Bring to me good fortune so that I may attract and share more fully with others.

An Invocation of Saturn

I invoke the power of Saturn into my life. Come to me strict and austere teacher. Help me build the forms that I desire. Teach me to accept and understand my personal circumstances. Help me grow in wisdom and fairness in all the ways of my life.

An Invocation of Uranus

I invoke the power of Uranus to radically change my life situation. Bring to me currents of divine freedom and openness. I seek your magnetic and all attractive energy to shatter past patterns and bring forth new and exciting developments into my life.

An Invocation of Neptune

I invoke the boundless and unfathomable Neptunian ocean. Help me to dissolve the erroneous patterns of my emotional life. Bring to me inspirational and uplifting spiritual experiences so that I may more fully appreciate and realize the Oneness and beauty of life.

An Invocation of Pluto

I invoke the transformative power of Pluto. I call forth your purifying and regenerative energy. Give me courage to honestly face myself and the power to transmute my self into my glorious Divine Self.

A Person-Centered Invocation

Let's create a person-centered invocation for an individual who has the Moon in Cancer in opposition to Mars in Sagittarius. The procedure is similar to that used in constructing aspect affirmations.

The Moon in Cancer is broken down into its component principles of receptivity, nurturing maternal energy, the feminine principle, caution, self-protection, and self-preservation.

Mars in Sagittarius correlates to our physical energy and action. Specifically, it relates to personal freedom, the future, and the metaphysical.

In combination, these planetary and zodiacal archetypes suggest an individual who can embody and express physical energy and action in terms of the feminine principle, receptivity, and self-protection. The energy flow emphasizes personal freedom and mental development. It also suggests a cautious and sensitive approach to achieving these goals.

Here are two invocations:

> *I invoke the lunar feminine principle of maternal and receptive love to aid my Mars energy in reaching my goals of personal freedom and physical strength.*

or

> *I invoke the power of Mars to aid me in all my endeavors so that I may practically care for my family and day by day express more feminine love to all with whom I am in contact.*

Pure Motive and Desire

Invocations and affirmations should always be said with absolute trust that the desired result or energy flow is taking place. Doubt, fear, and anxiety arising in our consciousness will tend to make the affirmation or invocation much less effective. Our subconscious mind cannot be fooled. Right motive is all important. Our pure desires and motives are the only protection we have against the misuse of these powerful techniques. If we call upon the energies of our soul and the powerful archetypes that surround and underpin all life, then absolute purity of intent is a prerequisite. Not only to reach the desired goal, but to do so in complete safety. If we display remnants of selfishness, greed, or other base desires in our choice of words or with our inner state while performing these techniques, then the forces affirmed or invoked will be of a base nature.

Affirmations and invocations are not in any way complex or difficult to use. The techniques are simply an extension of our everyday use (or misuse) of psycho-spiritual force. Every day we create and radiate emotion, thought and word power. Inexorably, we reap the harvest that we sow.

The prescribed techniques can help you to reprogram, purify, and dissipate erroneous emotional and mental patterns in your subconscious mind. As you walk the astrological pathway towards self-empowerment you become the transformative ground, the means, and the goal. You consciously reclaim your power day by day.

9

Zodiacal and Planetary Visualizations

Stars—the thoughts of God in the heavens.

—Longfellow

Visualization is one of the most powerful techniques we can use to transform our lives. Although it has recently become quite trendy to speak of creative visualization as if it's some new and innovative empowerment tool, visualization has been taught in the ancient mystical traditions for centuries.

The teaching is based upon the idea that the universe and all within it is visualized and thought into existence by the unwavering contemplation of the One Absolute Creator. Furthermore, in as much as we are a fragment of the One Life, it is said that we partake of the same gift for creative manifestation through the process of thought and visualization. Interestingly, modern theoretical physicists have recently come to the conclusion that the theories of natural phenomena, including the laws they describe, are more creations of the human mind—the result of our mental paradigm—rather than reality itself.

The inscription from the *Emerald Tablet*, "As above, so below," cryptically conveys the idea as does the concept of the heavenly man and the earthly man. Whether or not we accept this conceptual idea of the creative process of life, the fact remains that the conscious use of visualization has been an active ingredient in the lives of many successful people. In order to reclaim our power we should use any proven and safe technique that is not only relatively easy to use, but is tremendously effective. Visualization fulfills this criteria perfectly.

If we accept, as working hypotheses, the ideas that the zodiacal archetypes reside in the collective unconscious of humanity (as Carl Jung has stated), and that our specific planetary archetypes reside in our subconscious mind (as suggested in this text), it follows that by the conscious use of these archetypes in and through visualization techniques we are able to not only partake of the fundamental divine process that brings ideas into manifestation, but significantly we can do so in a way that our subconscious mind and the collective unconscious understands. This double-whammy approach brings far more positive therapeutic outcomes than can be expected from the normal application of visualization techniques.

A Conscious Approach

Sacred self-discovery through astrology definitely requires a conscious and balanced approach to life. If we are too emotionally volatile or lack the mental stability to ground ourselves while these techniques are being used, then the forces evoked can sometimes overwhelm our consciousness. This may result in us being thrown into greater mental, emotional, and spiritual turmoil. Therefore, it is wise to pause and assess our own peculiar situation and examine the psychic baggage that we carry. The use of high-voltage visualization, crystal energy, invocation, and affirmation techniques should only be undertaken when we have the requisite stability of self-conscious awareness.

Having taken care of the obligatory warning, here are some important hints to keep in mind when you practice your visualization exercises:

- Visualize as if you already have the object of your desire. In order to achieve something that we hunger for we should imagine that we already have it—see and feel it in your visual adventures. Also, believe that you are worthy to attain the changes in your life that you desire. In a very real sense it is not in the future—it's in the Eternal Now. Become a conscious cocreator and a joyous participant in your visual adventures.

- Do your chosen visualizations daily unless stated otherwise.

- Be precise and as creative as possible in your imaging.

- Always add emotional intensity to your visualizations.

Whole of Zodiac Breathing Exercise

To perform this exercise you will need to be somewhat familiar with the twelve signs of the zodiac, their glyphs, and archetypal meanings (see chapter 4).

This is a powerful exercise for developing a greater perception of the pure energy and potential within. If practiced over a period of months, it will free you from erroneous patterns of thought and it will eventually enable you to more fully radiate the true force of your own archetypal birth pattern.

Allow at least twenty minutes for this exercise and make sure you won't be interrupted. Repeat it no more than twice a week at first. Later, it can be interwoven with other techniques and repeated more regularly if you desire.

While relaxing in a chair or lying down, slow your breathing to a comfortable rate. Take long deep breaths, inhaling and exhaling rhythmically. Continue to focus on your breathing for a few minutes; feel the life breath entering into every atom of your being, revitalizing and healing your body. At this point you should be in a deeply relaxed and peaceful state, totally aware of yourself and enjoying your deep rhythmical breathing as the life-breath sweeps in upon you and is then slowly released. (Don't hold your breath during the period between inhalation and exhalation during any of these exercises.)

While breathing in, image a golden glyph of the zodiac sign Aries centered within a fiery circle. See it coming out of the distant darkness into your inner field of vision, then as the symbol is before your inner eye feel and see radiating from it pure Arian energy—the power of the germinating seed, the power inherent in all beginnings. Feel the energy enter you as you continue to breathe in. The seed-force of Aries circulates through every part of your being. Slowly exhale while retaining the Arian energy within you.

Repeat this procedure with the other eleven remaining signs of the zodiac, always seeing the golden glyph in the appropriate frame and feeling the force of the archetype as it permeates your consciousness. Fire signs are to be visualized in a fiery circle, earth signs encased in beautiful crystals, air signs amidst swirling winds, and water signs coming out of a clear pool of water.

After completing all twelve signs of the zodiac, you pulse with divine energy and vitality. You feel an inner fullness and completeness. Joy pervades you. Continue breathing rhythmically, aware that you embody both the parts and the whole. You are the beginning (Aries) and the end (Pisces) and the pathway between these signs.

Now, image the zodiacal energies merging within you. They form themselves into a pure white flame, incredibly small but as bright as the Sun. You can hardly look upon the blazing point of energy. It's centered in your heart. After a few moments consciously raise the blazing point of light so that it resides in your head. Next, while exhaling, start mentally radiating the totality of the zodiacal light in all directions from the center of your forehead. As you exhale, the blazing point of light expands and begins to fill all the space around you in all directions.

As you continue breathing in, pause as you watch the brilliant radiance spreading into the vastness of inner space then continue to let the energy go as you take your next exhalation. As this process comes to an end you see the radiance fade as it spreads out to infinity signaling the end of the exercise.

Planetary Rainbow Dance Exercise

To perform this exercise and the one that follows you will need to become familiar with the planetary symbols and their archetypal meanings (see chapter 5). The procedure is basically the same as for the whole of zodiac breathing exercise.

Do a few minutes of deep and rhythmic breathing and when you have entered into a relaxed and peaceful state visualize yourself standing on a beautiful silver floor. You stand strong and stable. You are immovable.

Next, image the planet Mars as a red fiery ball entering your field of awareness. Feel its raw power and strength as it surrounds your being. You feel energized as it merges in and through you. See the sphere of Mars transforming itself into a perfect arc like one shade of a rainbow. You are in the center of the arc which runs through your heart from either side of you with the ends resting on the silvery floor.

When you are quite comfortable with the Mars energy go through the same procedure with the following planets. First, Jupiter with its orange hue, then the Sun as a golden yellow disk, followed by Venus in emerald green, and finally Mercury as a blue sphere.

See and feel the rainbow arc of your planetary forces. You are in perfect control as you move around on the silver floor, dancing in rhythm with the rainbow of the planets. Let your hands manipulate the arcs. Move them in whatever way you desire. You are the Magician in perfect coordination and in perfect poise. You move effortlessly in the dance of life.

Next, while inhaling, visualize the rainbow turning upwards and forming itself into a circle with the top of your head, with the bottom of the circle still within your heart. Now, consciously send the individual planetary circles back to their source. One at a time, starting with Mars and ending with Mercury. As you release them they immediately revert back to beautiful planetary spheres before finally disappearing into the infinite vastness of your inner space. After releasing all of them, spend a few more moments in deep breathing before opening your eyes once again.

Planetary Aspect Balancing Visualization Exercise

This exercise is designed to help you to harmonize a specific part of your energy field by working with one planetary aspect at a time. The aspect you chose to work with should symbolize a specific area of your life that you desire to change.

The aspects in the birth chart symbolize the complexity of our psychology and our subconscious patterning. Any emotional or mental patterns symbolized by an aspect can be worked with. The so-called easy aspects (the trines and sextiles) often need to be energized into action. The dynamic aspects (the conjunctions, squares, and oppositions) usually correlate with modes of self-expression that need some refinement. The idea is to make changes in your subconscious mind by replacing an old pattern with a more positive life-enhancing one. Once again, you use language that the subconscious mind understands: gentle visual suggestions and symbols.

Any visualization exercise you perform can be tailored to your specific needs when the birth chart has been drawn. You will gain proficiency at both developing and doing the exercises with a little practice.

Let's take the example of a person who has Venus square Pluto in his or her birth chart. Quite often an individual with this aspect will experience severe blockages in the normal flow of relationships. The person with such an aspect often expresses compulsive sexual and emotional behavior in relationships. The following visualization exercise was made for a person with this pattern.

When doing planetary aspect balancing exercises, allow at least fifteen minutes and once again make sure you won't be interrupted. Repeat them no more than twice a week.

Venus-Pluto Aspect Balancing

While relaxing in a chair or lying down, slow your breathing to a comfortable rate and take long deep breaths, inhaling and exhaling rhythmically. Continue to focus on your breathing for the next few minutes, feeling the life-breath entering into your being, refreshing and revitalizing you. You should now be in a deeply relaxed and peaceful state, totally aware of yourself and enjoying your deep rhythmical breathing.

Now, visualize a beautiful emerald green sphere coming towards you from out of the distant vastness within. It is Venus—the archetype of pure love and creativity. As the sphere comes closer feel its harmonious, loving energy as it calmly radiates from Venus and engulfs you. Wave after wave of impersonal love stream down upon you and fill your being. You are literally bathed in the most soothing and secure love energy that you've ever experienced.

Now, when you are totally filled with the Venusian vibration, visualize a powerful and mysterious sphere circling just above your head. It is Pluto. You can sense the Plutonian energy as a magnetic and all-transforming stream of liquid violet light. The light is of a substance and power like you have never seen or felt before, but you trust it implicitly, knowing that you are a part of it and it seeks only the highest good for you.

Next, visualize Pluto's violet liquid light radiating in and through every atom of your body. You feel and see it merging with the beautiful emerald green of the Venus energy. It flows down to the depths of your being. Breath in deeply and mentally bless this beautiful new energy that now manifests as the deepest and most beautiful shade of emerald that you have ever seen.

When you are totally full and overflowing with the energy visualize both Pluto and Venus floating ever so gently and peacefully away from you. Slowly they recede back to the furthermost part of your inner vision, finally fading from sight once again. Open your eyes and feel the afterglow of the transforming power of pure love.

Invoking Your Solar Self

Your solar self is your inner guide and your holy guardian angel. By invoking our solar self we effortlessly raise our vibratory rate and purify our energy field.

Relax and breath deeply and rhythmically for a few minutes. When you are fully relaxed and at peace, visualize yourself within a golden yellow sphere. You are totally encapsulated within a beautiful and joyous bubble of solar energy.

Next, as you relax and enjoy the vibrant and creative energy of the yellow sphere, visualize an image of yourself sitting in front of you. However, this image is more like a god than you; he or she is a radiant being—your solar self.

See your solar self as perfect in all ways, and radiating peace, joy, clear intelligence, and pure love. Purple creative sparks fly out of the beautiful yellow aura of your solar self. They enter you and as they do you feel the blessedness of the energy fill your heart. Enter into a dialogue with your divine friend. Talk about your deepest needs and desires. Seek counsel and ask your solar self for guidance to help you in fulfilling your highest destiny.

After ten to fifteen minutes of most intimate conversation give thanks to your solar self and visualize him or her merging with you. You now pulsate with an amazing vitality, creative intelligence, and joyousness. An electromagnetic vibratory energy pervades you. You are now consciously aligned with your Higher Self, with the forces of evolution and with the powers of light and love.

Solar Uranian Visualization Exercise

The solar Uranian visualization exercise can be used to invoke radical change in your life. Prior to doing this exercise try to clearly formulate in your mind the kinds of changes you wish to see happen in your life. Be as precise as you can for in the exercise you will be invoking the power of Uranus to bring about these changes.

Allow at least fifteen minutes for this exercise and, as always, make sure you won't be interrupted. Repeat the exercise no more than twice a week.

While relaxing in a chair or lying down, slow your breathing to a comfortable rate and take long deep breaths inhaling and exhaling rhythmically. Continue to focus on your breathing for the next few minutes, feeling the life-breath entering into your being, refreshing and revitalizing you. You should be in a deeply relaxed and peaceful state totally aware of yourself and enjoying your deep rhythmical breathing.

As you contemplate the need for major changes in your life visualize a shaft of radiant white light coming into your body from above your head. It fills every fiber and atom of your body. It suffuses your consciousness with peace and joy. Next, see the beam of white light separate itself into two spheres. One is a beautiful amethyst, the other golden yellow. Both spheres pulsate with electromagnetic energy.

The golden yellow sphere symbolizes solar energy. It centers itself around your heart. Feel an openness in your heart and wait with expectation. The amethyst sphere is pure Uranian energy and is centered in and around your head. See an iridescent purple filling your head.

Now, while clearly imaging the two spheres invoke the following:

> *I [name], call upon the power of Uranus; I invoke radical transformative change in my life [state the specific area of your life that you want to change] so that I may more fully express [state clearly what you want to express] in my life.*

Repeat this invocation three times with tremendous emotional intensity. Say it with clear intent and a belief that the desired change is taking place. After a few minutes, visualize the two spheres of light once again becoming a single shaft of white light. However, this time the shaft of light merges within you and slowly fills every part of you.

10

Aspects and Crystal Energy Transformation

God, the true Philosopher's Stone,
Who answers every prayer,
Lies hidden deep within your heart,
The richest gem of all.

The subtle vibratory transformative power of crystals has long been known as one of the best aids for achieving changes within mind and body. For centuries the healing and protective qualities of crystals and gemstones (small, high-quality crystals) has been taught and practiced as part of both the Eastern and Western spiritual traditions.

It's hard to find a civilization that didn't prize the acquisition of a beautiful ring of emerald, lapis lazuli, ruby, or sapphire. From kings and queens to the ecclesiastical hierarchy, from the *Emerald Tablet* of Hermes to the exquisite symbolic jewelry of the Egyptians, from the ancient Greeks to the Romans to the Incas, from the North American Indians to the yogis of India—everywhere we see the use of crystalline energy.

Whether or not the wearer understands the inner significance, the fact remains that the collective unconscious of humanity is awash with crystal energy archetypes. More recently, the desire for lavish and expensive adornment has besotted the mind of modern man. Delusions of glamour and vanity have usurped the primal and more intrinsically important healing, transformational, and protective purposes that originally were so much a part of the use of crystals.

The wise have long recognized the electromagnetic effect on the body and mind by crystals and have sought to use them as aids in healing and body work. What is perhaps less known is that crystal energy can be used to change our subconscious patterning, as well as mitigate the potentially adverse effects of certain planetary cycles. The ancient Richis of India were experts in this field and some amazing stories abound in the literature of the Indian spiritual tradition about the healing power of crystals.

An understanding that the collective unconscious has been permeated with crystal archetypes gives us a clue to their great healing and therapeutic potential. Flowing out of this idea comes a significant realization: You can help transmute subconscious patterns of behavior by the use of the appropriate gemstone. You can also initiate the unfolding of seed-potential that lies just beneath the threshold of your consciousness.

Combining crystalline and planetary archetypes provides us with an interesting combination of transformative potential. The planetary archetypes are primarily concerned with our emotional and mental patterns, while crystal energy archetypes are high vibrational forces that provide a grounding point and a focus for energy to flow. They are, by their very nature, able to boost the energy field of whatever or whomever they contact.

However, crystals don't discriminate between increasing a positive or negative energy field. Once again, as in all techniques of personal empowerment and transformation, the onus is on the awareness and understanding of the participating individual. We need to make sure that we embody the requisite purity and right attitude.

Crystalline substances come under the rulership of Saturn. Saturn is the form builder and the initiator. He seeks the manifestation of spiritual and psychic energy. Saturn also symbolizes that auspicious moment in our cyclic development when we are asked to shatter our decaying bio-psychic forms.

Saturnian force, through its rulership of Capricorn, slowly and surely leads to the release and purification of the residue of our psychic energy. It initiates us into a new life pattern—symbolized first by Aquarius—with its concomitant group activity and its lessons of emotional and mental detachment, impersonal love and brother- and sisterhood. Secondly, we are initiated into the Piscean phase of the cycle with its desire for complete merging with the Source of All. The Piscean impulse to liberation and freedom from the past takes us out of a completed life cycle and into a new cycle of existence.

The question is, "How can we best use crystal energy and planetary symbolism to affect life-enhancing changes in our subconscious mind that will enable us to express all that we are capable of being?" The short answer is to use any practical and coherent technique or method that uses the appropriate crystalline force and relates directly to our seed-pattern of life, as symbolically shown in our birth chart.

Many highly technical and convoluted methods can be constructed to realize this objective. However, the simplest and most symbolically correct methods are preferable. Some of these methods are detailed below. As there are many books that detail the care, purification and inner meanings of crystals these subjects won't be discussed in our necessarily brief exploration of astrological aspects and crystal energy transformational techniques.

Gemstone Planetary Rings

The first technique is really very simple. It involves wearing a gemstone or combination of stones and metals on a particular finger. The choice of stone, finger, and metal is dependent upon, and correlates to, your planetary aspects at birth.

Traditionally, all the planets and signs of the zodiac relate to particular gemstones. This has led to the practice of wearing birthstone rings. For example, a Sun in Leo person may wear a citrine or yellow sapphire ring, whereas a Sun in Aries person may wear a garnet or ruby ring.

There is no authoritative and definitive guide to the relationship between gemstones, planets, and signs. Different authors in the field suggest very different correlations. However, the following tables will assist you in choosing the appropriate stone(s) for yourself. If you find you have a preference for a particular stone that isn't listed or one that happens to correlate to a different planet or sign just follow your intuition. Trust your Higher Self.

Table 9. Gemstones, Metals, and the Planets

Planet	Symbol	Gemstone	Metal
Sun	☉	Yellow Topaz and Sapphire	Gold
Moon	☽	Moonstone	Silver
Mercury	☿	Opal	Mercury
Venus	♀	Emerald and Green Tourmaline	Copper
Mars	♂	Ruby	Iron
Jupiter	♃	Sapphire	Tin
Saturn	♄	Diamond	Lead
Uranus	♅	Amethyst	
Neptune	♆	Aquamarine	
Pluto	♇	Garnet	

Table 10. Gemstones and the Signs of the Zodiac

Sign	Symbol	Gemstone	Metal
Aries	♈	Ruby	Iron
Taurus	♉	Emerald	Copper
Gemini	♊	Opal	Mercury
Cancer	♋	Moonstone	Silver
Leo	♌	Yellow Topaz and Sapphire	Gold
Virgo	♍	Jade and Agate	Nickel
Libra	♎	Green Tourmaline	Bronze
Scorpio	♏	Garnet	Steel
Sagittarius	♐	Sapphire and Lapis Lazuli	Tin
Capricorn	♑	Diamond and Turquoise	Lead
Aquarius	♒	Amethyst	Aluminum
Pisces	♓	Aquamarine	Platinum

It's not just a matter of choosing a gemstone that relates to your Sun sign. This is an oversimplification of the practice in the same way that newspaper "star signs" are a crude caricature of astrology. In our use of crystal energy and astrology we will add a little more complexity and power by moving beyond Sun-sign techniques, yet at the same time we won't get lost in a labyrinth of technicality.

As earlier stated, another way of choosing a stone is to use your intuition. You may feel intuitively that you need to wear a particular stone or you may be given one. For example, if you feel a strong desire to wear an aquamarine or if someone suddenly gives you one, consider its relevance to your present circumstances and whether or not it resonates with you at a deep level.

In the same way that the various gemstones and crystals relate to specific planets and signs, so it is that each of our fingers relates to a particular planetary force. Furthermore, the right and left hands symbolize our conscious and subconscious expressions respectively (for a right-handed person).

All that remains is for you to determine what particular life issue you desire to work with and then locate the appropriate chart aspect that most clearly symbolizes that issue. (You will learn to do this in the next chapter.)

For example, let's imagine that you are having difficulty in your relationships with unresolved anger. Suppose your birth chart has a Sun square or opposition Mars aspect. In this instance you could have a ring made in gold with a yellow sapphire or citrine and a ruby set into the top at an angle of either 60 or 120 degrees (sextile or trine aspect) to symbolize harmony of the energies.

The idea of wearing the ring is to send a clear message to your conscious and subconscious minds that says you are ready and willing to transmute this particular part of yourself.

Polarity Gemstone Rings

You can also enhance the quality of your energy field by wearing a gemstone that embodies an energy diametrically opposed to a troublesome psychological aspect pattern that you have. In the case just described, you could wear a silver emerald ring on your right hand to emphasize your desire to consciously express energies of a more loving and harmonious nature.

Some notable spiritual masters have stated that gemstones should be of at least two carats in weight in order for the electromagnetic effect to take place. It's preferable that this hint be taken up wherever possible, but in many cases the cost may well be prohibitive—especially when several stones are needed. In this instance a smaller, high quality stone will suffice as quality may well be as important as size.

Wherever possible, gemstones should be worn so that they touch your skin. To ensure this happens, you will have to instruct your jeweler to make sure that the stone is set low enough to touch your finger when the ring is worn.

Gemstone Talismans

The same kind of effect can be achieved by the use of pendants and other talismanic pieces of jewelry. In the case of a talisman the scope for symbolizing planetary aspects is much greater due to the increased surface area of the piece.

The sheer size of a talisman makes it possible to symbolize not one but several themes in our life. The talisman becomes a living vibrational symbol of our individuality that slowly and imperceptibly helps release us from the effects of debilitating subconscious patterns.

When we combine the use of talismans with affirmations and invocations, as well as visualization techniques, we have an incredibly powerful armory at our disposal to regenerate our being. All these methods and techniques blend in together beautifully. They provide a seamless approach to the process of self-discovery and empowerment.

Creating Your Own Jewelry

The art of the goldsmith and the process of forging metal is both primal and intrinsically satisfying at a deep level. The combination of intense heat, water, precious metals, beautiful gemstones, and creativity can be quite spellbinding. While it's unlikely that all who read this book will have the opportunity to learn these techniques firsthand, it is strongly suggested that any effort put into the construction of your own rings or talismans will be well rewarded.

Not only will you have consciously decided what parts of yourself you want to regenerate but you will have participated directly in the creative process by designing and crafting your own individualized jewelry piece. In this instance, the effect on your consciousness is bound to be even more pronounced.

Crystal Empowerment and Manifestation Exercise

This very simple exercise can be done when you are feeling tired, enervated, or lacking in inner peace and joy. It's also helpful when you desire to begin a new enterprise or accomplish something big. You will need two wands of clear quartz crystal or alternatively any two of your favorite crystal wands.

Sit with your arms by your sides holding the crystals. Then, visualize a current of electromagnetic energy starting to vibrate around your body. Imagine that you can feel the energy (pretend if necessary). It starts around your feet and slowly moves up your body until it's all around you. Next, move your arms so that your right hand wand points skyward while your left hand wand points to the ground.

Now, internally or out loud call upon the power of the crystal to enter you and aid you in manifesting whatever you desire—energy, joy, a relationship, a new career, etc. Remember that crystals are ruled by Saturn, the form builder, the archetype of bringing things into concrete manifestation.

When you intuitively feel an energy transfer has taken place, give thanks to the crystalline forces invoked and mentally direct the energy through the left hand crystal wand into the ground. This is symbolic of grounding the energy so as to achieve the dynamic results you desire. Repeat this exercise as frequently as desired.

11

Finding the Major Themes
in Your Birth Chart

Astrology is astronomy brought to Earth and applied to the affairs of men.

—Ralph Waldo Emerson

Before you can begin to practice the psycho-spiritual techniques of the astrology of self-empowerment, i.e., affirmation, invocation, visualization, and crystal energy transformation, you will need to learn how to locate the major themes in your birth chart.

While there's a widespread perception that astrology is an incredibly complex art that requires many years of study and practice in order to gain proficiency, finding the major themes in a birth chart is a relatively straightforward exercise if certain basic rules are followed. There's no denying that certain aspects of astrology are complex and highly technical, but it's still possible to convey the fundamental concepts and ideas involved in a relatively uncomplicated way.

As we have seen in previous chapters, the basic astrological language consists of the twelve signs of the zodiac, the ten planets, and their interrelationships at the moment of birth.

If we simplify our approach and focus on the most outstanding planetary and zodiacal factors, finding the major themes in our chart becomes simply a matter of following the prescribed rules. To help you get the most out of this chapter, it's suggested that you write down the themes on a piece of paper as you work your way through the text.

The major themes in your birth chart are symbolized by:

- Your ascendant and first-house planets.

- The ruler of your chart by sign and house position.

- Your Sun and Moon (the Lights) by sign and house position.

- Your major dynamic aspects.

- Planets conjunct the angles.

Now, let's examine each one of these factors in more depth and look at a few sample charts. When you understand the concept involved you are ready to look at your own birth chart and write down the appropriate details.

Your Ascendant and First-House Planets

Chapter 6 describes in detail the inner meaning and role the ascendant plays in our overall psychology. Before continuing, you may like to refresh your understanding of the ascendant by rereading relevant parts of that chapter.

Once your birth chart has been calculated spotting the ascendant and any first house planets is a breeze. Simply by looking at the left-hand side of the birth chart you will see the sign of the ascendant; it sometimes has the abbreviation "asc" beside it. First-house planets are just as easy to find. The first house is usually numbered—just note any planets located in this house.

Your ascendant and first house planets provide the first keys to unlocking the celestial code of your life potential. These factors alone provide amazing insight into your most natural form of self-expression. They also indicate possible blockages in the free flow of your vital energy. (Aspects to the ascendant as well as aspects in general will be covered later in this chapter.)

In the sample chart (see figure 4), the ascendant is Pisces. There are no first house planets. Now, look at your own birth chart. Find your ascendant and note any first house planets, then write down the details. If you do not yet have your birth chart, there are a variety of computerized services available that can quickly calculate your chart (see the free natal chart offer at the end of the book).

Your Ruler: By Sign and House Position

The ruler is a very ancient concept in astrology. Originally, the ruler was called the "lord" of the birth chart. The lord not only presided over our birth but also oversaw our entire life. Such was the power of the lord in ancient astrology that it was considered almost a deity, appointed by the Universal Life, to look after our unfolding life according to divine plan.

The ruler's position, by sign, house, and aspect, is an important symbol of our destiny and potentiality. It beautifully symbolizes our general orientation and field of life experience. Finding your ruler is just a matter of determining what planet rules your ascendant and then locating what sign and house it's in.

In the sample chart the ruler is Neptune and is found in Scorpio on the cusp of the ninth house. Now, look at your own birth chart. Find your ruler (the planet that rules your ascendant or rising sign) and note its sign and house position.

Your Sun and Moon by Sign and House

The meaning of the Sun and Moon has been covered in chapter 5. To locate the Sun and the Moon by sign and house is, once again, very easy.

In the sample chart the Sun is in Libra in the eighth house, while the Moon is in Leo in the sixth house. Now, look at your own birth

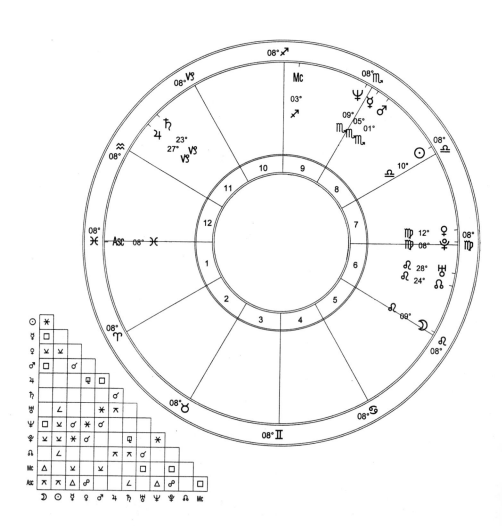

Figure 4. Natal Chart: 4 P.M., October 4, 1961, Invercargill, New Zealand

chart. Find your Sun and Moon and write down the details of their sign and house positions.

Your Major Dynamic Aspects

For the purposes of transformational astrology we will look for the following major dynamic aspects in your birth chart and construct exercises and therapies around them. Allow an orb, or allowance from exactness, of 10 degrees for the major dynamic aspects (see also chapter 7). The major dynamic aspects are:

- the conjunction (0 degrees).

- the square (90 degrees).

- the opposition (180 degrees).

Should your birth chart not have any of these aspects then the following minor dynamic aspects may be worked with instead. Allow an orb of 3 degrees for minor aspects. The minor dynamic aspects are:

- the semi-sextile (30 degrees).

- the sesquiquadrate (135 degrees).

- the quincunx (150 degrees).

A computer-generated birth chart may include all the above aspects in table form (see figure 4). However, if your chart doesn't have the aspects already calculated you can do it yourself. Count around the 360 degrees of the zodiac circle, looking for the three major dynamic aspects. These aspects are relatively easy to find. A few examples will help you get the idea.

In the sample chart see if you can see the following aspects:

- the Moon square Mars, Mercury, and Neptune.

- Venus conjunct Pluto.

- Mercury conjunct Mars and Neptune.

- Mars conjunct Neptune.

Now, look at your own birth chart and write down the major dynamic aspects.

Planets Conjunct the Angles

A planet is said to be angular when it's conjunct the angles of the birth chart. The angles are the ascendant, the midheaven (abbreviated *MC* in the sample charts) and their opposite points in the birth chart. An angular planet, particularly if it falls in the first or tenth houses, makes its presence felt very powerfully in your life.

Any planet conjunct an angle (the ascendant-descendant axis or the MC-IC axis) is very powerfully positioned and needs special attention in the analysis of your birth chart. Even if the planet is in your twelfth house, provided it's conjunct the ascendant, it will always symbolize a major theme or dynamic energy flow in your life. Such a planet may even dominate the ascendant energies if it's powerfully aspected.

Finding planets conjunct your angles is simply a matter of looking at the angles and noting any planet within ten degrees of the angle.

In the sample chart the following planets are conjunct the angles:

- Pluto in the seventh house.

- Venus in the seventh house.

- Uranus in the sixth house.

Now, note any planets in your own birth chart that are conjunct the angles. With the information gathered you are now ready to create your own unique astrological self-empowerment program. However, if you are still having difficulty finding the major themes in your birth chart you may like to look at the following example and go through the procedure again (see figure 5).

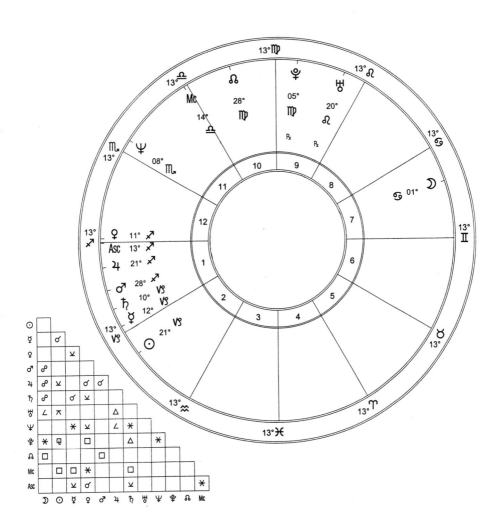

Figure 5. Natal Chart: 5:30 A.M., January 12, 1960, London, England

As noted earlier in this chapter, the major themes of a birth chart are symbolized by:

- The ascendant and any first-house planets.

- The ruler of the chart—by sign and house position.

- The Sun and the Moon by sign and house position.

- The major dynamic aspects.

- Planets conjunct the angles.

In the sample chart:

- The ascendant is Sagittarius. Jupiter, Mars, Saturn, and Mercury are in the first house.

- The ruler is Jupiter and it's conjunct the ascendant in the first house.

- The Sun is in Capricorn in the second house. The Moon is in Cancer in the seventh house.

The major dynamic aspects are:

- The Moon opposing Mars, Saturn, and Jupiter.

- Mercury conjunct Saturn.

- Venus conjunct Jupiter and square Pluto.

- Mars conjunct Jupiter.

Planets conjunct the angles are:

- Venus and Jupiter.

12

Creating Your Program for Self-Change

And for that love, the mighty yogis practice yoga from age to age;
When love awakes, the Lord, like a magnet, draws to Him the soul.
—from an ancient Hindu text

Throughout the preceding chapters you have been introduced to the astrology of self-empowerment and learned the specific techniques of transformation and self-empowerment that are to be used. In the last chapter you located the major themes of your birth chart and now all that remains is for you to choose one or two areas of your life that you desire to work on and build a program of exercises around them.

This chapter shows you how to take your major themes and use them to create the exercises that will help empower you. It's a matter of personal preference which particular techniques you use although a combination of therapies will bring about very dynamic results.

For example, affirmations are excellent, even on their own, but when you combine them with visualization or crystal energy techniques then an even greater potency of transformative energy is set in motion.

Let's pause and recap for a moment. There are five steps that lead to astrological self-empowerment. These are the steps that ultimately allow us to reclaim our Sacred Power and manifest our highest destiny. By following these steps we will tend to naturally express our highest birth chart potential.

- Step one involved developing an understanding of astrological self-empowerment. This included learning about the signs, planets, houses, and aspects and their part in the practice of Sacred Astrology.

- Step two introduced the specific techniques of the astrology of self-empowerment, including affirmation, invocation, visualization, and crystal energy transformation. These are the techniques that help you to make fundamental changes in your psycho-spiritual nature.

- Step three taught you how to find the major themes and potentials in your birth chart.

- Step four is the design of your personalized astrological program of self-change centered upon your major themes, patterns, and inner potentiality. At this point in the process you must decide which areas of your life you wish to work on. You also choose specific exercises and therapies from those provided (affirmations, invocations, visualizations, and crystal energy therapies) or you create your own personalized exercises and therapies.

- Step five is the ongoing practice of the techniques of Sacred Astrology.

We are now, of course, at step four. It's time for you to look at the themes of your birth chart and decide which features and patterns (as symbolized by aspects, angular planets, the Sun or Moon positions, etc.) you wish to work with. In making these decisions remember that the most important thing is your intuitive feeling about what needs changing in your life.

For example, if deep in your heart of hearts you desire to change your relationship pattern (even though others may think your relationship is just fine) look for themes involving either your seventh house or Venus' position and aspects. Always flow with your intuitive response and trust in the process.

How to Create Your Program

Let's look at a sample birth chart given in the preceding chapter (see figure 4). We found the following major themes in the chart.

- **Ascendant and First House:** Pisces ascendant with no planets in the first house.

- **Ruler:** The ruler is Neptune in Scorpio in the ninth house.

- **The Sun and the Moon:** The Sun is in the eighth house in Libra, while the Moon is in Leo in the sixth house.

- **Dynamic Aspects:** The Moon square Mars, Mercury, and Neptune; Venus conjunct Pluto; Mercury conjunct Mars and Neptune; Mars conjunct Neptune.

- **Planets Conjunct the Angles:** Pluto in the seventh house, Venus in the seventh house, and Uranus in the sixth house.

While this person has several themes that could conceivably be worked with, one stands out (this is usually the case) as being highly dramatic and problematical. It's clear that this individual has a major confrontation with the use of personal power, will, and force (Scorpio and Pluto prominent with the Sun in the eighth house; the Moon square Mars, Mercury, and Neptune; ruler conjunct Mars).

This kind of astrological configuration suggests a life full of trauma, change, and difficult experiences. Certainly this individual's life reflects the birth chart mandala. As an archetypal symbol of this person's life struggle and potentiality, it is remarkably accurate.

For this person, exercises involving these dynamic placements would be a great place to start, particularly if this individual is ready to confront unresolved anger, manipulative tendencies, jealousy, possessiveness, and use of personal power generally.

The following program could be used as a beginning to self-discovery and transmutation.

A Sample Astrological Self-Empowerment Program

Affirmations:

> *I am loved and I know how to love.*
>
> *I transform my life with dynamic willpower.*
>
> *I am always ready to begin again.*
>
> *I purify myself day by day.*

Do these affirmations daily as many times as desired (see also affirmations for Pluto and Scorpio in chapter 8).

Invocations:

> *I invoke the mighty transformative power of Pluto to help me purify my consciousness. Help me love and accept all others and myself. As your force enters me I feel the remnants of anger, fear, insecurity, and jealousy dissolving into poise, peace, acceptance, and total understanding.*

Say the invocation three times once daily.

Visualization Exercises:

> Practice the whole of zodiac breathing, invoking your solar self, and rainbow planetary dance visualization exercises.

Crystal:

> Have a silver ring with an opal and ruby made. This is to symbolize the Moon-Mars-Mercury-Neptune configuration. Wear it on your right hand to symbolize self-conscious control of these forces.

Let's look at the second sample chart (see figure 5). The major themes in this chart are represented by:

- **Ascendant and First House:** Sagittarius ascendant with Jupiter, Mars, Saturn, and Mercury in the first house.

- **Ruler:** The ruler is Jupiter in Sagittarius and is found in the first house.

- **The Sun and the Moon:** The Sun is in the second house in Capricorn, while the Moon is in Cancer in the seventh house.

- **Dynamic Aspects:** The Moon opposing Mars, Saturn, and Jupiter; Mercury conjunct Saturn; Venus conjunct Jupiter and square Pluto; Mars conjunct Jupiter.

- **Planets Conjunct the Angles:** Jupiter in the first house and Venus in the twelfth house.

This person faces a major confrontation with his or her ego and sense of self (first-house emphasis), self-confidence or lack of it (Capricorn Sun and Mercury conjunct Saturn), the use of the sexual energy and relationship patterns (Venus very prominent on ascendant square Pluto). This person also must learn many lessons involving patience, self-sacrifice, and loyalty (the Moon opposing Mars, Saturn, and Jupiter), as well as lessons involving the right use of resources (second-house Sun highly aspected).

For this individual, exercises and therapies that tackle these issues would, naturally, be highly beneficial.

The following program could be used as a beginning to self-empowerment and transmutation.

A Sample Astrological Self-Empowerment Program

Affirmations:

> *I build wondrous forms to share with others.*
>
> *I stand strong and confident.*
>
> *I am attractive and radiate magnetic power.*
>
> *I see the Divine in all forms.*

Do these affirmations daily as many times as desired.

Invocations:

> *I invoke the power of Saturn to help me learn the lessons of self-lessness, patience, loyalty, and responsibility. I seek your wisdom to help me build beautiful forms and learn the lessons of my life.*

Say the invocation three times once daily.

Visualization Exercises:

> Practice the whole of zodiac breathing, rainbow planetary dance, and Venus-Pluto balancing visualization exercises each once weekly.

Crystal:

> Have a gold ring with an emerald and ruby made. This is to symbolize the balancing of the Venus-Mars sexual energy.

It's now time for you to create your own unique program of self-change. It's not as hard as you might think, now that you have discovered the major themes in your chart. To inspire and aid you in the final leg of the journey here are a few hints and key statements.

As you create and practice your program of Sacred Astrology:

- Motive is all important. Try to be pure in your desires, but especially so when doing your exercises.

- Keep affirmations simple, precise, and positive.

- Repeat affirmations and invocations daily.

- Always expect the most positive outcome.

- Put emotional feeling and intensity into your practice. As you call upon the powers of the zodiacal and planetary archetypes, put your heart and soul into it.

- Try to be creative and anticipate rapid results.

- If results are not immediate keep at it. Never give up on the process of divine transmutation.

- Timing is critical so be patient. The long-sought-after moment of pure joy, pure inspiration, or pure transfiguration will come. It is your destiny to receive all these gifts and more.

- A program of self-change doesn't have to be arduous and time consuming. One simple but powerfully intoned affirmation can create a vital, new life-enhancing pattern in your consciousness. So don't think you need to be too clever. Keep it simple and you will be amazed at the positive results you receive.

- The Universal Forces are eager to aid you in your process of change, but you must call upon them.

- Above all else, seek the grace of God.

As you weave the magic of sacred soul alchemy, remember:

- You can't go wrong. Don't worry about making mistakes. All your seeming miscalculations, failures, and errors of judgment are but steps along the way to the manifestation of your highest destiny.

- Sacred Astrology is meant to be a joyous and exciting process. As always, trust in the process. You are always being guided by your Higher Self.

- You are a divine archetype in time and space and, as such, you fulfill a need of this moment. The need of the moment automatically invokes the solution.

- As you call upon the forces of the Universal order and attempt to reclaim your Sacred Power you live a truly authentic life that is aligned to the archetypal patterns of your core being.

So, we are nearing the end of this book on Sacred Astrology. As you travel upon your astrological voyage of self-discovery may celestial beings accompany and dance with you and may your journey as a star-light alchemist be filled with magic, inspiration, and joyous alchemy. May your highest and purest desires radiate forth and may the Great Shining One guide you onwards in all the ways of your life.

Love, light, peace, and wisdom to all.

Epilogue

Astrology is an incredible gift given to us by the Universal Intelligence to aid in the unfolding of harmony, order, and beauty in our lives. It's founded upon the archetypal forces of the zodiac and the planets. Most miraculous of all, it speaks in its beautiful and sacred symbolic language, the code of the stars, of a synchronistic relationship between celestial phenomena and our unfolding life pattern.

Like all gifts, astrology can be misused or neglected. Yet, the opportunity is ever with us, and when astrology is used wisely it becomes one of our finest psycho-spiritual transformative techniques. It becomes a spiritual alchemy of symbolic living.

The planets and the signs of the zodiac eternally convey their message of hope and meaning in a world that sorely needs such meaning. Silently and faithfully the stars radiate their cosmic message. They speak of an existence beyond our comprehension, and they embody loving and compassionate modes of being that we are all reaching towards.

The way to reclaim our power through astrology is the way of the heart and the way of understanding. It's achieved by each of us consciously realigning ourselves to the creative love-force of life. If we truly reach for the stars with our hearts and souls then we shall surely fulfill our highest destiny and become star-light beings.

Glossary

air signs. Gemini, Libra, and Aquarius.

angles. The most sensitive and influential points of the birth chart. The cusps of the first, fourth, seventh, and tenth houses (except in the equal house system).

angular houses. The first, fourth, seventh, and tenth houses of the birth chart.

ascendant. The zodiacal degree rising over the eastern horizon at the time of birth. Each degree changes at approximately four minute intervals. Also called the *rising sign*—the cusp of the first house.

aspect. The angular relationships formed between planets and house cusps as seen from the earth.

astro therapist. The astrological equivalent of a psychotherapist.

birth chart. The horoscope, natal chart, or chart.

conjunction. An aspect formed when two celestial bodies pass each other on the same point of the ecliptic.

cusp. The lines dividing the houses of the birth chart. For example, the beginning of the first house is called the *first house cusp.*

descendant. The opposing point to the ascendant. The cusp of the seventh house.

earth signs. Taurus, Virgo, and Capricorn.

ecliptic. The apparent path of the Sun through the sky.

elements. Fire, earth, air, and water are the four elements of astrology.

elevated planets. A planet takes on more power and significance if it is elevated, i.e., if it is located near the midheaven.

esoteric. Metaphysical teachings known only to a select few or to the initiated.

fire signs. Aries, Leo, and Sagittarius.

fixed signs. Taurus, Leo, Scorpio, and Aquarius.

horoscope. The natal chart or birth chart.

houses. The twelve divisions of the birth chart.

Imum Coeli (IC). The point of the birth chart opposing the midheaven (MC).

lights. The Sun and the Moon.

Medium Coeli (MC). The midheaven.

opposition. An aspect of 180 degrees between two planets.

orb. An allowable range of influence in determining an aspect.

progressions. A method for determining the cyclic development of an individual.

rising planet. A planet situated close to the ascendant.

ruler. The planet that rules the ascendant; also called the *lord* of the chart.

sextile. An aspect of 60 degrees between two planets.

signs. The twelve signs of the zodiac.

square. A 90 degree aspect between planets.

transit. The position of a planet in the celestial sky at the present point in time as it relates to our birth chart. Transits are an important tool for determining the phase of life development we are in.

trine. An aspect of 120 degrees between two planets.

water signs. Cancer, Scorpio, and Pisces.

zodiac. The band of sky 18 degrees wide that has as its central line the ecliptic. It consists of twelve signs, each 30 degrees wide.

Index

fire, 27–30, 36, 44, 60, 66, 110, 128, 162
first house, 73, 75–77, 144–145, 150, 153, 155, 161
first-house planets, 77, 144, 150
Fish, 50–51
fixed, 18, 27, 48, 162
flowing aspects, 85–86, 90
fourth house, 75, 78
freedom, xvii, 7, 29, 35, 48–49, 62, 71, 80, 83, 92, 94, 107, 117, 121–123, 137

G

Gemini, 25–27, 32–33, 35, 43–44, 55, 58, 102, 111, 138, 161
gemstone, 136–140
Goat, 46
gods, 58, 62, 66
gold, 113–114, 138–139, 156
grace, xviii, 8–9, 11, 50, 87–88, 157
Great Mother, 34, 50, 112
guilt, 41, 43, 64, 70

H

Hades, 70
hard lessons, 65
healing, xii, 8, 21, 70, 117, 127, 135–136
health, 39, 76, 79, 84
Hermes, 58, 73, 135
hero, 60, 86, 104, 121
higher learning, 81
higher Self, xiv, 87, 132, 138, 158
horoscopes, xii
houses, 7, 20, 73–84, 148, 152, 161–162
humanity, xi–xii, 6, 23, 40, 45, 48–49, 126, 135

I

ideals, 41, 44, 48, 69, 82
identity, xi–xii, 37, 50, 74, 77, 79
illumination, 15, 67
initiator, 64, 136
inner meaning, 12, 18, 144
inner process, 87, 93
inner space, 54, 128–129
integration, xv, 3, 6, 14, 24, 54, 60, 68,

78, 85, 90–91, 95
intellectual faculty, 28
intellectual stimulus, 33, 77
intuitive or unconscious response, 57
invocation, xiii, 20, 92, 96–97, 119–123, 126, 133, 143, 152, 154, 156
invoking your solar self, 131, 154

J

jealousy, 70, 154
Jewel of Eternity, 13, 113
Jupiter, 44, 54–55, 62–64, 105, 121, 129, 138, 150, 155

L

Lao-tzu, 19
lapis lazuli, 135, 138
law, 81, 84
leadership, 37
Leo, 25–27, 36–38, 40, 43, 46, 49, 55–56, 100, 112, 137–138, 145, 153, 162
Libra, 25–27, 39–44, 55, 59, 103, 114, 138, 145, 153, 161
Light of Life, xv, xvii
Lights, 112, 144, 162
Lion, 36, 38
love, xiv–xv, 3, 26, 30, 32, 34, 47–48, 50–51, 59, 62, 69, 79–80, 83–84, 94, 101, 103, 107–108, 112, 114–115, 117–118, 121, 123, 131–132, 137, 151, 154, 158
love and harmony, 80, 118
lunar cycle, 57

M

magician, 33, 129
magnetism, 77
major dynamic aspects, 144, 147
mandala, xviii, 23–24, 153
mantle, 37
mantra, 97
Mars, 28, 54–55, 60–62, 71, 92, 104, 121–123, 129, 138–139, 147–148, 150, 153, 155
mastery, 38–39, 78
matrix of individuality, 8
mental blockages, 86

☽ REACH FOR THE MOON

Llewellyn publishes hundreds of books on your favorite subjects! To get these exciting books, check your local bookstore or order them directly from Llewellyn.

ORDER BY PHONE

- Call toll-free within the U.S. and Canada, 1-800-THE MOON
- In Minnesota, call (651) 291-1970
- We accept VISA, MasterCard, and American Express

ORDER BY MAIL

- Send the full price of your order (MN residents add 7% sales tax) in U.S. funds, plus postage & handling to:

    Llewellyn Worldwide
    P.O. Box 64383, Dept. K644-0
    St. Paul, MN 55164–0383, U.S.A.

POSTAGE & HANDLING

(For the U.S., Canada, and Mexico)

- $4.00 for orders $15.00 and under
- $5.00 for orders over $15.00
- No charge for orders over $100.00

We ship UPS in the continental United States. We ship standard mail to P.O. boxes. Orders shipped to Alaska, Hawaii, the Virgin Islands, and Puerto Rico are sent first-class mail. Orders shipped to Canada and Mexico are sent surface mail.

International orders: Airmail—add freight equal to price of each book to the total price of order, plus $5.00 for each non-book item (audio tapes, etc.).

Surface mail—Add $1.00 per item.

Allow 2 weeks for delivery on all orders.
Postage and handling rates subject to change.

DISCOUNTS

We offer a 20% discount to group leaders or agents. You must order a minimum of 5 copies of the same book to get our special quantity price.

FREE CATALOG

Get a free copy of our color catalog, *New Worlds of Mind and Spirit*. Subscribe for just $10.00 in the United States and Canada ($30.00 overseas, airmail). Many bookstores carry *New Worlds*—ask for it!

Visit our website at www.llewellyn.com for more information.

Symbols of the Soul

Discovering Your Karma Through Astrology

GINA LAKE

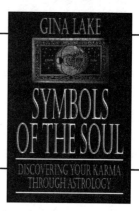

Astrology's symbols are the soul's language of life. They reveal not only the mysteries of the universe, but also the mysteries of each person's life. They are unlimited resources for psycho-spiritual insight, revealing our soul's agenda for this lifetime and the personality chosen to carry it out.

If you've ever wondered what issues you brought into this lifetime from other lifetimes, what your life purpose is, how your Sun sign and Moon sign are serving your evolution, and what your life lessons are, *Symbols of the Soul* will give you the tools to answer these important questions. You will learn how to synthesize the information from Saturn, the Moon's Nodes, the Sun and Moon signs, and the aspects to understand how karma is manifesting in your life.

1-56718-407-3
6 x 9, 264 pp., illus. $12.95

For Readers of

Astrology for Self-Empowerment

only

FREE Natal Chart Offer

Thank you for purchasing *Astrology for Self-Empowerment*. There are a number of ways to construct a chart wheel. The easiest way, of course, is by computer, and that's why we are giving you this one-time offer of a free natal chart. This extremely accurate chart will provide you with a great deal of information about yourself. Once you receive a chart from us, *Astrology for Self-Empowerment* will provide everything you need to know to interpret your chart's potential.

Also, by ordering your free chart, you will be enrolled in Llewellyn's Birthday Club! From now on, you can get any of Llewellyn's astrology reports for 25% off when you order within one month of your birthday! Just write "Birthday Club" on your order form or mention it when ordering by phone. As if that wasn't enough, we will mail you a FREE copy of our book *What Astrology Can Do for You!* Go for it!

Complete this form with your accurate birth data and mail it to us today. Enjoy your adventure in self-discovery through astrology!

Do not photocopy this form. Only this original will be accepted.
Please Print

Full Name:_____

Mailing Address:_____

City, State, Zip:_____

Birth time:_____ A.M. P.M. (please circle)

Month:_____ Day:_____ Year:_____

Birthplace (city, county, state, country):

_____

_____

Check your birth certificate for the most accurate information.

Complete and mail this form to: Llewellyn Publications, Special Chart Offer, P.O. Box 64383, K644–0, St. Paul, MN 55164.

Allow 4-6 weeks for delivery